I0518562

PRAISE FOR WIN ONE WON
— WHAT CHAMPIONS ARE SAYING —

"If you want to be inspired and motivated as a coach, athlete, or simply someone with a desire to be successful in chasing your dreams—read Coach Wingreen's book, *Win One Won!* It will help you to understand the necessity of developing a strong work ethic."

- Dick Vitale, ESPN
Naismith Basketball Hall of Fame, Emmy Award

"*Win One Won* serves as a powerful reminder that true success lies in our daily mindset and discipline. Andrew Wingreen offers a compelling framework that leaders can apply across all arenas—whether in sports, business, or everyday life."

- Mark Batterson, National Community Church
New York Times Bestselling Author

"*Win One Won* is more than a leadership fable. . . it's a mindset shift. If you're in the business of building people, you'll want this in your locker room and your life."

- Donnie Jones, Head Men's Basketball Coach, Stetson
2x NCAA National Champion, Florida

"I've known Andrew for over a decade now and continue to be super impressed with his love for the game and love for people. His intentionality when it comes to development is exceptional. Having had the privilege to be in coaching for over three decades, I know the importance of living in your true identity. I'm certain those that read this book will capture Andrew's heart for influencing others to find the best version of themselves."

- Ritchie McKay, Head Men's Basketball Coach, Liberty
2019 Jim Phelan National Coach of the Year

"In *Win One Won*, Andrew Wingreen provides insights into a powerful framework that transcends the court and applies to every aspect of life. His message is both simple and deeply impactful: winning isn't merely an outcome, but a consistent way of showing up in every moment. Through *Win One Won*, Andrew masterfully teaches individuals and teams how to approach each day with intention, empowering them to "win the day, the mission, and the mindset." This book is a must-read for anyone looking to develop leaders, cultivate a stronger culture, or elevate their team's performance. Coach Wingreen's ability to deliver high-energy, story-driven, and intensely practical wisdom shines through every page, equipping readers with the tangible tools needed to grow, lead, and win, time and time again."

- Tony Miller, Asst. Men's Basketball Coach, Bob Jones
Founder of A Quick Timeout

"What an inspiring journey that Andrew takes us on as we follow Jai through his high school and collegiate career. The lessons learned at each stop are pivotal for any athlete looking to become the best they can become. Evolving and growing is a process-oriented journey, and in *Win One Won*, we get to see each step. This is a wonderful read for any young athlete regardless of sport. The lessons here are as much about life as they are about basketball."

- Bob Starkey, Asst. Women's Basketball Coach, LSU
NCAA National Champion, LSU

"Andrew Wingreen is a friend of mine and we coached together. He's a fabulous husband and a terrific dad to his two beautiful girls. I read *Win One Won*, closed my eyes and I thought I was reading one of my dear friends, Joshua Medcalf's books. I've done podcasts for each of Joshua's bestselling books, *Chop Wood, Carry Water* and *Finish Empty*! This is a book for every coach and player. The coaching lessons in this book are timeless! I'm proud of you, Andrew, and I can't wait to do the podcast!"

- Brendan Suhr, Founder/CEO of Coaching U
2x NBA World Champion, Detroit Pistons

WIN ONE WON

WIN ONE WON

WIN EVERY MOMENT, ONE DAY AT A TIME

ANDREW WINGREEN

WIN ONE WON

ISBNs:

979-8-9994703-0-0 *Paperback*

979-8-9994703-1-7 *Hardback*

Published by:

Wingreen Publishing

To my wife,

You inspire me every day and shine bright through the chaos.
You've been a light all these years and I'm so grateful for you!
I love you.

To my daughters,

Thank you for always elevating the energy in the room and
bringing joy to so many!
I love you.

CONTENTS

INTRODUCTION

Everyone wants to win. Few understand how.

We live in a world that celebrates the highlight reel. The final shot. The big trophy. The viral moment.

But the truth is, winning doesn't begin on the scoreboard. It begins long before anyone is watching. It starts in the shadows. In the unnoticed effort. In the daily decisions. In the unseen habits that stack up over time.

This is the story of a young athlete named Jai. On the surface, he had all the tools—talent, athleticism, ambition.

But what he didn't yet have was the mindset and heartset to sustain success. Like many, he thought greatness came from skill. But real greatness? It comes from who you become.

Win One Won is a mindset. A call to action for every competitor, leader, and dreamer to rethink what it means to win.

In these pages, you'll walk with Jai through setbacks, lessons, and breakthroughs as he learns to:

Win the moment with intentional habits and preparation.

Embrace the power of **One,** one day at a time. The adversity, the growth, and the resilience required to rise.

Discover what it means to have truly **Won.** When success turns into significance, and impact becomes your legacy.

This story isn't just about sports or business. It's about life and becoming better through the process.

By the end, you'll see that winning isn't about the outcome, but about the legacy your life leaves.

And you don't have to wait for the championship to start living it.

Let's begin.
One moment at a time.

PART ONE
WHERE IT ALL BEGINS
THE ADVENTURE TO LEGACY AND SIGNIFICANCE

ONE
EVERYONE SEES THE
FINISH LINE

Jai was in the moment. The arena lights were bright, casting a glow on the hardwood floor while the game clock read 0:12. There was a buzz among the fans, who couldn't believe what they had just witnessed. After all, Jai's team was the underdog and had come from behind to take a seven-point lead. Jai could hardly believe it himself. "We are going to win. We are actually going to win!"

The reality was finally sinking in. Minutes earlier, Jai had dived on the floor for a loose ball, securing a crucial possession that sealed the game. But this wasn't just any game, this was the national championship. For the first time in school history, they were about to bring home the trophy. To say this was a huge deal would be an understatement.

Jai had always been one of the best players on his team, but in the most important game of the season and of his college career, he struggled to score. In years past, this would have destroyed his confidence and put him in a negative frame of mind. But this year was different. This season and this game, he was able to embrace a new mindset.

In previous seasons, Jai and his teammates had tasted success, but they could never quite get over the hump and reach their ultimate goal. Their efforts were never quite enough, which always bothered Jai. He used to wonder why it always ended the same way, why his teams fell just short, and what it would take to finally break through.

But not today. Today Jai was about to accomplish the goal he'd always dreamed of—winning a national championship!

Although only twelve seconds remained, it seemed like an eternity for the players and coaches on the court. They knew what was about to happen, but they had to wait just a little longer.

As one of Jai's teammates knocked down the final two free throws, the arena erupted. The ball was inbounded and the crowd began to countdown. The urgency and excitement from the fans was palpable.

"5, 4, 3 . . ."

The players on the bench held each other back while the ball was being dribbled out.

"2, 1 . . ."

The final buzzer sounded. Confetti blasted into the air, and a celebration erupted like no other. Everyone, players and fans alike, lost their minds!

Grown men cried, mothers hugged everyone in sight, and the players jumped, shouted, and high-fived. They had won the national championship in truly the upset of the century.

Jai couldn't help but smile and shake his head in disbelief. He knew exactly what it took to reach this moment and all the people who had poured into him over the last several years. He took a moment to soak it all in because from the outside looking in, most people would have thought it came easy. But deep inside, Jai knew the grind this journey had been and the work he'd put in to get his mindset and heartset in the right place.

Everyone saw the victory. But few would ever understand the countless hours, the setbacks, and the transformation it had required for Jai to get here.

After the trophy presentation and all the media fanfare had subsided, Jai took a moment to himself, bowed his head, and thanked God for all the blessings in his life, giving Him all the glory.

The trophy sparkled under the arena lights, and a championship banner would hang in the rafters forever. But for Jai, the real prize wasn't the outcome. It was the transformation he'd earned. The adventure had reshaped his mindset and revealed who he was always meant to become.

As the noise quieted and the confetti settled, he remembered where this journey had all begun. His mind went back to the first time he'd heard the phrase:

Win One Won.

Little did he know back then . . . just how much this phrase would change everything.

TWO
TALENT ISN'T ENOUGH

Growing up, Jai and his family were all about basketball. He was around the game nonstop, whether going to a high school game his uncle was coaching, attending a middle school girl's game to see his aunt coach, or conversing about ball at a holiday party. Besides that, much of his free time was spent playing the game himself.

Jai was full of energy and dreams. On his nightstand sat a small sign with a quote from Walt Disney:

"IF YOU CAN DREAM IT, YOU CAN DO IT."

He believed that. Deep down, he thought anything was possible.

Most nights, he'd lie in bed flicking the ball into the air, working on his form and follow-through. If the spin wasn't perfect, the rep didn't count. Ball *really* was life.

In the winter, when snow blanketed the ground and the air stung with cold, Jai still found a way to get shots up. His process was simple:

- Shovel driveway
- Fill the bathtub with hot water
- Rotate between two basketballs

When one ball froze and lost air, he'd dunk it in the tub, dry off the other, and keep going. Back and forth, switching balls, battling the cold and the clock until a neighbor finally yelled for him to wrap it up.

Even then, Jai couldn't end without a game-winner. If he missed, he was obviously fouled. So he stepped to the line, crowd roaring in his mind, and sank the free throws. That's how the night would end.

He had been around the game his whole life and put in more hours than most. But for all the passion and practice, Jai still struggled with the one thing that held everything together. The mindset to reach his full potential.

Talent was never his issue. In fact, Jai made a name for himself as one of the top players in the area when, as a freshman in high school, he dropped 32 points in a varsity game. The opponent was a rival from across town, and Jai was called up due to a short-handed roster. He was incredibly nervous but knew he was a good player. He came off the bench and hit four consecutive three-point shots to catapult his team to a 12–0 run. The entire gym couldn't believe what they were witnessing!

As exciting as that moment was for Jai, it unknowingly instilled an arrogance inside of him that disguised itself as confidence. It didn't help that everyone talked him up and told him how big of a deal he was. His family was there to keep him humble, but the attention he received from teachers and his friends at school made him feel unstoppable.

During his freshman year, Jai believed raw talent was all he needed. He showed flashes of brilliance, but without structure or discipline, bad habits crept in fast. The coach rarely intervened. Now and then, he'd raise his voice or pretend to lay down the law, but it never stuck. The team saw right through it. He wasn't invested, and they felt it. Accountability only showed up when the scoreboard didn't go their way. By then, it was performative. Jai and his teammates learned early that under this coach, effort and attitude didn't matter unless they were losing. And by then, the damage had already been done.

Over the next two seasons, Jai started to show up late to practice every now and then. The team practiced early in the morning, but Jai was *not* a morning person. He would set his alarm to get up in plenty of time to make it to practice. However, the snooze button became Jai's best friend and won him over too many times.

After two seasons of inconsistent effort and little accountability, Jai was eager for something to change. That change came at the start of his junior year, when the program brought in a new head coach. Jai wouldn't know it then, but this transition would be the beginning of his adventure into the *Win One Won* mentality.

———

Coach Victor was an older gentleman, maybe in his late sixties or early seventies. He and his wife had just moved into town from across the country where he had been a high school basketball coach for thirty years. Over the years, Coach Victor had amassed over six hundred wins and won three state titles. While his accomplishments in the game of basketball were worthy of the hall of fame, his real genius was developing championship team cultures.

After a quick Google search, Jai could tell Coach Victor was the real deal. There were numerous newspaper articles written about his teams and all the success they had. Jai was even able to watch some old media interviews where Coach Victor spoke about his journey in coaching and why his teams thrived. The way Coach Victor talked was different that anything Jai had experienced so far in his life.

In one of Coach Victor's vintage interviews the reporter asked, "What two aspects of coaching have led to your success as a coach?"

He answered boldly and confidently, "Our staff coaches the player's heart more than their body, and we value culture more than any plays or strategy."

Jai was excited to have a new coach, but he quickly realized he was going to need to change. At the very first team meeting, Coach Victor began by saying, "We are going to change everything about this program. The way we show up every day needs to be different. I've heard stories about the culture of this team and how many of you believe your talent is good enough to win championships. I love that we have talented individuals. That is a must. But if we are going to accomplish the goals we have as a team, we will need to win every day. This isn't about you. This is about the team."

The team appreciated the fresh tone their new coach brought, but most of them didn't fully understand what it would take to "win every day."

For Jai, this season wasn't just about wins or stats. It was the start of something deeper. A shift toward consistency, effort, and accountability. Whether he realized it or not, his mindset was about to change forever.

THREE
WHEN PURPOSE FINDS YOU

Coach Victor was a successful coach. Everyone could see that. His résumé preceded him, and he was well-known and liked by almost everyone he met. When people would look at his career and see all the wins and championships he'd accumulated, they would be in awe and say things like,

"What a lucky guy" or "What would it be like to have won as much as he has?"

Well, rewind the tape thirty-plus years.

What most people didn't understand was that Coach Victor hadn't always been successful. No. In fact, Coach Victor hadn't even begun his coaching career until he was thirty-six years old.

Before he was "Coach Victor," he was just Victor. Before coaching he had worked several jobs, including as a manager of a retail store, a truck driver, and even a year or two flipping burgers at McDonald's. He never went to college and even spent time unemployed because of layoffs. To say the least, Coach Victor didn't have it easy.

While he was always grateful for God's provision and the jobs he did have, he knew his calling in life was something bigger. Something that would impact people and show them the significance they could have in their own lives.

That longing eventually turned into prayer. Daily, desperate, expectant prayer.

Then one snowy morning, he stumbled into a free community leadership workshop out of sheer curiosity. He didn't know it then, but it was the divine interruption he'd been praying for. There, he met a retired high school coach who casually mentioned his old school was looking for a new coach—volunteer only, no pay, and likely no wins either.

Coaching had never piqued Victor's interest before, but something tugged at his heart during this conversation. He wasn't sure if it was the lunch he had just eaten or if it was a purpose of something greater, but Coach Victor couldn't stop thinking about pursuing this coaching "job."

Days passed, and this interest turned into an obsession. Victor couldn't shake the idea of coaching basketball and knew this was an opportunity God was calling him to. He had worked his entire life chasing something bigger, something better, and here it was. This was it.

He always believed if he did things the right way and did them consistently, he would be rewarded. He had seen so many people talk about success and want it so bad, but they would never take action or do the steps necessary to achieve that success. Coach Victor wasn't about to fall into that trap, so he immediately picked up the phone and expressed his desire to be the new basketball coach. The school district was desperate, so it didn't take much convincing to get him hired! But he knew if he could help a few kids believe in themselves the way he was beginning to believe in himself, it would be worth it.

This move would change the trajectory of Coach Victor's life and ultimately, the lives of so many.

That first season of coaching was rough. More losses than wins, more questions than answers. But it was also when a simple truth began to take root: You don't win everything at once. You win the moment in front of you. And then the next. And then the next.

It was during those late nights and early practices of his coaching career that the *Win One Won* philosophy was born. Over the next thirty plus years, that strategy became a system. That system became a standard. And that standard became the foundation for every team he would ever lead.

FOUR
THE WAKE-UP CALL

F ast-forward back to the present day, and Coach Victor was excited to begin a fresh adventure at his new school. While many people referred to life as a journey, he preferred the word *adventure*:

"Journeys you go on by yourself, but adventures you go on with people you love."

There was a pep in his step, and he exuded joy.

At the first team meeting, Coach Victor noticed one of the last players to walk in was Jai. He glanced at his watch—one minute late. Coach Victor had already heard that Jai was one of the most talented players on the roster, and this moment confirmed what he suspected. This young man wasn't used to being held to a standard. From the way Jai strolled in, it was clear he didn't think punctuality mattered, especially with a new coach who probably seemed like just another old guy just passing through.

"Glad you could join us, son," Coach Victor said. "I watched film and can clearly see you're as talented of a player as they come.. I look forward to catching up with you after the team meeting."

The team didn't know this yet, but Coach Victor was a stickler for punctuality. He was a firm believer if you didn't show up at least seven minutes early, you were late.

< 7 MINUTES EARLY = LATE

———

Jai's confidence was boosted! He sat through the entire meeting thinking about all the stats he was going to post this upcoming season, completely tuning out Coach Victor's message. Team culture, team rules, decorum, blah, blah, blah. Obviously this stuff wasn't important and wouldn't apply to Jai or his teammates. I mean, he'd heard all of this before from the previous coaching staff, but no one ever meant what they said. So back to daydreaming it was for Jai until dismissal time.

Jai couldn't wait to talk with Coach Victor afterward, excited to get his ego stroked by this new coach.

This guy has won everywhere he's been, but he's never had a player like me! We are going to win so much, and I'm going to be the star! Jai thought.

———

Finally the meeting ended. Jai approached Coach Victor, "Coach! We are going to win a lot of games this year! I can't wait to—"

"Why were you late to the meeting?" Before Jai could finish his sentence, Coach Victor interrupted him with boldness and concern.

Jai was caught off guard and started to say, "What do you mean? I was only a minute late! I was finishing up a conversation with a friend and figured I'd make it on time."

Coach Victor wasn't amused and knew it was time to make an impact on Jai. He was hoping Jai would have taken ownership for being late, but unfortunately that didn't cross Jai's mind.

"You're the most talented individual on this team. It's clear as day. But if you don't build the habits that can help you sustain your talent, you'll never reach your potential as a player or as a person. Showing up late sends a message, but the bigger concern is what it reveals: a failure to hold yourself accountable and honor your commitment to the team. You need to be better. Now I don't know you very well yet, but I know you well enough to tell you I believe in you. I trust that you want to be the best, and I'm going to help you become the best if you remain coachable and open to change. Are you up for the challenge?"

Jai crossed his arms, leaning against the locker with an offended demeanor. "So what? Do you think being late one time means I'm not committed?" he snapped.

Coach Victor didn't flinch. He stood calm and steady, eyes locked on Jai with quiet conviction. "It's not about being late once. It's about what that says to your teammates, and more importantly, to yourself."

Jai looked away, still tense. "My last coach didn't care," he muttered. "I did what I wanted and still got buckets."

"And where did that get you?" Coach asked, voice calm but firm.

Silence.

Jai shifted uncomfortably. He wanted to argue, but deep down he knew Coach Victor was right. He'd felt it in the pit of his stomach ever since the season started. Something was off. It wasn't about the game anymore. It was about who he was becoming. Or maybe, who he wasn't.

Coach continued, "You've got talent, Jai. But talent won't carry you where you want to go. What will, is learning to win every moment, especially the ones no one sees. That starts with the simple stuff. Like being on time."

Jai stayed quiet. He didn't like the feeling of being held accountable and his body language made that point very clear.

Coach stepped a little closer. He knew that the people hardest to love are often the ones who need it most. "Look, Jai, I'm not here to tear you down. I'm here because I believe in who you can become. But you've got to want it too. So tell me, do you want to stay stuck in your old habits, or do you want to grow into something greater?"

Jai took a deep breath and uncrossed his arms.

"My last coach let me get away with everything," he admitted, finally making eye contact with Coach Victor. "I'm sorry I was late. I don't know how to build better habits yet, but I do want to be the best and I think you can help me."

Coach Victor smiled. "Good. Then let's start with showing up, on time, every day. That's where we begin."

"Meet me in my office tomorrow morning at seven o'clock. We will lay the foundation to a philosophy I call *Win One Won*. Bring a pen and a notebook and be ready to write down some notes. If you ink what you think, you will recall these lessons ten times better."

Coach Victor knew that the hardest people to love are the ones that need to be loved the most, and he was going to do just that.

FIVE
PEN, PAPER, AND PURPOSE

I t's seven o'clock, Coach! I made it here on time!"

"I'm proud of you, Jai! That's a big step in the right direction." Coach Victor was glad Jai was punctual, but he knew deep down that being on time was barely scratching the surface of all the principles Jai would need to learn in order to be the best. However, Coach also knew he had to celebrate wins when they occurred, and the process to Jai's growth wasn't going to happen all at once. If anything, Coach now knew Jai was serious and he was willing to improve.

"Did you bring your pen and notebook?" Coach Victor asked. "We're about to dive deep into the *Win One Won philosophy.*"

23

"Yep," Jai said. "My parents never give me money to spend on stuff, but after I explained our conversation to them, they took me to the store and said I needed something nice to write with. Oh, and I asked them to give me a ride today to make sure I was on time. They seemed pretty excited I had a meeting with you today!"

"That is awesome! I'm sure they are very proud of you, Jai." Coach said.

"This mindset of *Win One Won* is going to take time to fully grasp, and that's okay," Coach Victor said. "It took me years to learn, and to be honest, I'm still learning how to live it out every day. But I want to help you avoid the mistakes I made so you can go further, faster."

He paused for a moment, then continued. "I remember working through this with a player a lot like you when I was a younger coach. He got it. Now he's a head coach at the college level, and a really good one. I see that same potential in you, Jai. So let's not waste a minute. Open your notebook and write this down:"

WHAT LEADS TO WINNING?

"Now what do you think the answer to that is?" Coach Victor was curious to see how Jai viewed winning.

"Scoring points?" Jai answered. "Um . . . working out every day. Going to practice. Shoot, Coach. This is hard!"

Coach Victor stopped him with a chuckle. "I mean, those things are all important. You can't win without practice and scoring points, but let's dig in a little deeper."

Jai leaned in and nodded his head. "Okay."

"If we know practice is important and scoring points is needed, how do we make sure we can do those things at a high level?"

Jai let out an audible sigh. "Coach, you're killing me with all these questions. It's only 7 a.m. I'm still half asleep."

"You said you wanted to be the best, right?" Coach asked.

"Yes. I do, Coach," Jai replied. "Okay. If I wanted to score points I guess I would need to practice my shot more and get more reps. I'd probably need to work on my finishing around the rim too."

"Great! This is a good start. Let me ask you another question to dig a little deeper."

Coach Victor was a master at going for the gold. He never settled for one-word answers and always prodded a little more to get those he was interacting with to think with purpose.

He continued to pepper Jai with questions, both to continue the conversation and to spark new thoughts. "I agree. Repetitions are important. But how do you ensure you are able to plan and execute the proper practice to make those repetitions count?"

"I guess I need to develop better habits," Jai said.

"Exactly. Habits are the things you do every day that lead to winning. You can't just magically snap your fingers and find success. Talent is great, but it's never enough. Your habits will take you to all the places you want to go." Coach Victor's wisdom astounded Jai. "For you and for this team to win, we need to first start by winning every moment, every day."

Everyone wants to win. Few understand how.

Jai stared at the floor. He had a nervous bounce in his knees that made it clear his mind was spinning.

In the past, Jai had tried to implement better habits. He knew what needed to be done, but failed to consistently execute his processes and systems. He was fearful of trying again, because he didn't want to be known as a failure.

Coach Victor watched him carefully. "You're quiet, Jai. What's going on in that head of yours?"

Jai hesitated, then shrugged. "I don't know . . . just thinking, I guess."

Coach pulled over a chair and sat down across from him. "You've got that look like the weight of the world just landed on your shoulders."

Jai cracked a weak smile, but it didn't last long. "I'm just trying to figure it all out. It feels like a lot."

"A lot?"

Jai nodded slowly.

Coach leaned in. "Is it the pressure? Feeling like you've got to be perfect? Win every moment?"

Jai looked up at Coach. He felt a relief as if he knew the battle that was raging inside of him.

"Yeah," Jai finally said. "That. I feel like if I mess up even once, I'm losing. Like I've already failed."

Coach nodded. "That's normal. But that's not what *Win One Won* is about, Jai. You're not expected to win *every* moment, you're expected to show up for them. Learn from them. Keep going."

Jai exhaled. "That sounds a little better."

"It is," Coach said with a small grin. "We're not chasing perfection. We're building purpose. One moment at a time."

"That seems like a lot to take in, Coach." Jai seemed a little overwhelmed by what Coach Victor was saying. "I feel a lot of pressure needing to win every moment of my life."

"I understand your concern, Jai, but I promise you we will simplify this process so you can be successful. Once you engrain the *Win One Won* mindset into your brain, it will become second nature. Get ready to take notes."

To be great, you'll need to fall in love with the process.

PART TWO
WIN
WIN EVERY MOMENT, EVERY DAY

SIX
CHOOSE TO WIN

Most days, Jai was nonchalant about school or practice. He generally got away with coasting through life without anyone really pushing him to get better. In all fairness, Jai didn't realize he was lacking in some crucial leadership abilities. In his mind he was doing the best he could, but he also knew he wanted more. He wanted to be a better friend, a better teammate, and a better example to everyone around him.

It didn't take long for Jai to receive his first lesson in his *Win One Won* adventure. As the season began, the team opened up against a cross-town rival, or at least a team that used to be a rival. Their opponent hadn't been very good in its recent history and Jai had always had big games against them. In fact, the last time Jai's school lost to this team was over fifteen years ago. Nobody, including Jai, felt this would be much of a game at all.

Jai and his teammates approached the days leading up to the "easy win" with a lot of goofing around and a lack of focus. The next game after this one would be against a team who'd made the state tournament last season, so the guys even began to talk and prepare for *that* game, thinking the one against the bad team didn't matter.

Coach Victor kept reminding his players that winning was a choice. All that mattered was the next game and to keep the mentality of 1–0. 1-0 meant all they should care about was winning the next game. Nothing else. Everyone had to make a sacrifice for the betterment of the team. Coach knew in order to do this, they needed to focus on winning the moment each and every day. Coach explained how winning the moment is about presence, not perfection. It's the choice to own what's in front of you, right now, with your full attention and best effort. However, getting that point across to a bunch of immature high school kids was harder than it looked.

WINNING IS A CHOICE.

The day before the so-called "not important game," Jai was talking to some of his teammates after practice.

"Dude, how many points do you think I will score tomorrow?" he said with a little chuckle. "I haven't even watched film on these guys and I'm feeling like it will be an easy thirty points."

A couple seniors on the team, who were all a part of the previous culture, egged on Jai and jumped right in.

"Thirty? That's it? Don't you remember last year how bad we beat them? They lost their leading scorer too. Man, if you don't score forty points we're going to have to say you stink," they laughed.

"Bet," said Jai with a smirk. "Just give me the ball all night tomorrow and watch."

Unseen by Jai and his teammates, Coach Victor had walked into the gym and overheard this exuberant and foolish conversation. Now, Coach Victor was typically pretty calm, but he was also old school and was never afraid to show some tough love to his players. He cared more about their growth as young men than he did about winning the game.

To say the least, Coach Victor was not happy. "I've never heard such a losing conversation in my life! I've been coaching for over thirty years and have been around a lot of teams, but somehow, someway, I've never had the opportunity to hear such arrogance toward an opponent."

As upset as Coach Victor was, he also felt hurt because not too long ago he had his office meeting with Jai where they had gone over the *Win One Won* mindset. He believed the whole team was beginning to turn the corner, but Jai's arrogance was bringing everyone down.

"Jai," said Coach. "A word?"

"Sure, Coach."

"Meet me in my office in five minutes."

"Jai, did you retain any of the information we spoke about? Just last week you said you were ready to level up your habits. Do you remember going over what a winning mentality looks like? Do you still want to be the best, or was that just a lot of talk?"

"Coach, I was just joking around about how many points I'll score."

Coach Victor knew this was an opportunity for a teaching moment with his best player.

"The way you approach each moment is what separates you in sports and in life. As I told you in the office, this is something we will be working on over time. I don't expect you to have this perfect. You can never achieve success in one day, but you can do the things that lead to it daily. If you truly want to be great, you need to change your approach and do a better job locking in. Do you still have your notebook that you took all those notes down with?"

"Yeah." Jai was still unable to fully embrace a coachable spirit, but knew he wanted more. "I want to be great and I'm glad you're helping me out. Yes, I still have the notes from our meeting."

"Remember, winning is a choice. We choose to win when we do the right things, day after day. It's the way you show up and how your carry yourself. When you go home, I want you to look over those notes and let me know your thoughts tomorrow morning. In fact, I will have you present some of them to the entire team before our game because I think everyone could benefit from this."

As soon as Jai got home, he went straight to his room to find that sacred notebook. He opened it up and began to recall in vivid detail all the things Coach Victor had taught him.

SEVEN
THE WINNER'S APPROACH

Jai sat on the edge of his bed with his notebook in hand. He hadn't opened it up or taken any notes in weeks, which is maybe why he's been acting out lately. It seemed like an eternity since that warm day in the summer when he sat down with Coach Victor and discussed the type of player he wanted to become. Jai thought he grasped the *Win One Won* philosophy back then, but after today's wake-up call, he knew he hadn't been living it.

Things at home weren't easy either. Like many high schoolers, Jai found himself in constant arguments with his parents. It wasn't anything major, but he couldn't shake the feeling that they "just didn't get him." Instead of leaning into their support, Jai slipped into a victim mindset, overlooking the fact that the people who loved him most were actually in his corner.

He instantly began to regret how he had been acting. He wanted nothing more than to be the best player and earn a scholarship to play in college. It's not that he was refusing to implement the *Win One Won* philosophy, he just simply hadn't had enough practice with it yet.

As he flipped open the worn notebook, he was struck by his own words he had written: "WIN: Win every moment, every day." He had little notes everywhere, but in bold right beneath that quote he had scribbled down the phrase "But to win the moment, you must be in the moment."

The words from Coach Victor had lived rent-free in Jai's head as if they had been waiting specifically for this night to speak.

He was motivated more than ever to show people he was different. He knew talk was cheap and decided in that moment he was going to be disciplined to lead his team to new heights.

Okay, he thought. *Let's see if I can remember what Coach Victor talked to me about last summer.*

It didn't take long before everything came back to him. He replayed that meeting in his mind as he read his notes and began to reconstruct his mindset into something better.

Jai scanned through the pages of his notes and there it was— Coach Victor's list, written in bold across the whiteboard that summer:

- **How you show up matters.**
- **Your attitude sets the tone.**
- **Your energy elevates (E²) others.**
- **Your effort reflects your personal standard.**
- **Your focus builds unshakable confidence.**

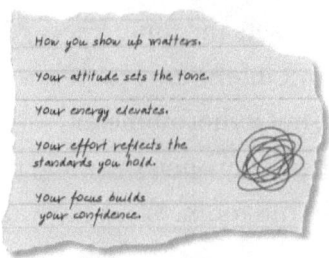

These weren't just words. They were the foundation of something deeper: the Winner's Approach.

It was more than motivation. The way you show up each day, your attitude, energy, effort, and focus, was the difference between hoping to win and preparing to win.

It was like Jai was reading this for the first time. He whispered to himself, "I have been missing this all along."

———

- **Show Up (The Winner's Approach)** - The way you walk into a room matters. Studies have shown that first impressions are formed in the first thirty seconds and often as soon as three to seven seconds. It's crucial to show up with the right attitude, energy, effort, and focus.
- **Attitude** - This walks into the room before you do. Be positive. Say hello to people. Have a smile on your face.
- **Energy** - This sets the tone. Energy Elevates, or E^2, is all about intentional presence. Be a thermostat, not a thermometer.
- **Effort** - Talent may open the door, but effort keeps you in the room. Work hard and be efficient.

- **Focus** - Be where your feet are. To win the moment, you must be in the moment.

———————

He thought about how poorly he had showed up to practice that day. He had taken his opportunity for granted and treated the day like it didn't matter. He'd reverted back to old habits of thinking talent alone was enough to keep him at the top of his game. But he realized it wasn't. This wasn't how he was going to lead a team to the next level, and it surely wasn't how he was going to land a scholarship to play in college.

He remembered how Coach Victor had called the Winner's Approach the foundation of champions. How champions are built by the way they show up, long before tipoff. The attitude you bring with you into every room matters. The effort you give in any task you are given matters.

Your approach matters.

It's about how you prepare and the routines you adhere to every day. It's the processes and systems you have in place to perform at the highest level possible.

Coach's speech echoed in his head:

"Anyone can talk about winning," Coach had said, "but very few know how to prepare for it. Champions win the unseen moments. They win the dark hours when nobody is watching. They win when it's inconvenient. That's the Winner's Approach.

"Success doesn't come from bursts of energy every once in a while," Coach had said. "You can't reach your goals if you only work on the days you feel good. Success comes from being intentional in everything you do. It's a conscious decision to show up with the right approach even when it doesn't feel convenient. You need to own it.

"A winner's approach is built before you ever step foot into the arena," Coach Victor said. "It's how you walk into every room. It's how you respond to coaching. Your mastery is created by your consistency. What you do every day matters."

Jai sat there on his bed in silence. He felt like he'd been punched in the chest as the conviction of not living up to the standard hit him. He knew it wasn't a matter of his ability, but that of his approach.

He quickly flipped back to the five traits Coach Victor had had him write down and underlined them in bold. He proceeded to write down one sentence for each to hold himself accountable to a higher standard.

> I WILL SHOW UP EARLY AND BE LOCKED IN.
>
> I WILL HAVE A POSITIVE ATTITUDE AND BE COACHABLE EVERY DAY, EVEN WHEN THINGS DON'T GO MY WAY.
>
> I KNOW ENERGY ELEVATES. I WILL BRING ENERGY THAT IS CONTAGIOUS TO EVERYONE AROUND ME.
>
> I WILL GIVE 100 PERCENT IN EVERY REP, EVERY DAY.
>
> I WILL STAY FOCUSED ON THE MOMENT AND CONTROL WHAT I CAN.

As he looked over again what he'd written, he put his pen to paper to write one more line.

> IT'S NOT ABOUT PERFECTION. IT'S ABOUT APPROACHING EVERY DAY WITH AN INTENTION TO LIVE UP TO THE STANDARD.

Jai was able to lay his head on his pillow peacefully that night. He wasn't just going to sleep with a new goal or desired outcome, but rather he was embodying a renewed mindset. He couldn't wait to go to practice the next day and prove he was better than what he had been showing recently.

The following morning Jai woke up rejuvenated and excited. He didn't even have to hit the snooze button on his alarm. He put on some of his favorite music as he got ready and prepared his heart and his mind for the day ahead of him.

He didn't feel like he had to chase success anymore. Instead, he understood he was building it, one day at a time. Every action he took was playing a role in shaping his future, and he was set on winning each and every one of those actions.

For the first time in a long time, Jai felt like he was approaching the day the right way. He felt in control.

EIGHT
WINS IN THE DARK

J ai always wanted to be ready. The game had always come so easy to him. His talent consistently led to personal success, but it had never translated to team success. After speaking with Coach Victor and meeting one-on-one for several sessions, he was beginning to understand why his habits and routines made a difference. He was ready to take his preparation to new heights.

He started showing up differently. Not louder or flashier, just ... more present. He was at least seven minutes early to film sessions. He began to ask better questions in practice to help the team grow. He made it a point to encourage his teammates, regardless of the situation. While he still wasn't perfect, he was striving to be consistent. He began to know his role and was stepping into it.

Consistency had been the theme of *Win One Won* so far, and Jai believed he could put what he'd learned into practice. And over time, his consistency began to compound into confidence.

After a long day of school and practice, Jai was always tired and would typically spend his evenings playing video games or scrolling through NBA highlights on TikTok. He climbed the stairs to his room, turned on his gaming system, and sat down to play. His friends were ready to play, too, but Jai remembered the promise he'd made to himself earlier that day that he was going to write and prepare before he played. It was time for him to decide what he was going to do.

As much as he anticipated playing NBA 2K with his boys, Jai made a difficult decision to turn off the game and open up his notebook instead. It didn't feel right, he reminded himself to trust the process. He remembered the wisdom Coach Victor shared with him:

"Never sacrifice what you want most for what you want at the moment."

Okay. I'd rather be playing video games, but I know that's not what I want most. This isn't what I want to do in the moment, but I know it's what I need to do, he thought. *In fact, I get to do this, and I'm going to trust that this process will help me achieve my goals.*

It was time for Jai to just do it.

Jai grabbed his pen and began to write down his wins from the day. It was a practice Coach Victor had taught him months ago, but one he had never followed through on. He had learned how writing down everything that went well for him that day would build his positive muscles in his brain and allow himself to focus his attention on doing those things again.

THIS. I AM PROUD OF THE CHOICE I MADE TO PREPARE FOR MY DAY INSTEAD OF PLAYING VIDEO GAMES. I DID A GREAT JOB OF LISTENING AND LEARNING FROM MY COACH TODAY. IT'S BEEN OVERWHELMING, BUT TODAY I REALLY FELT LIKE I WAS GROWING AND GETTING THE HANG OF THINGS.

WINS IN THE DARK WILL ALLOW ME TO CONSISTENTLY SHINE IN THE LIGHT.

Jai closed his notebook. Although he'd only written down two wins from his day, he was overtaken by joy and accomplishment. With a big smile on his face, he turned his attention to tomorrow. An eagerness was building inside him that he hadn't experienced before. He thought about how he was going to wake up, what he was going to wear, and how he was going to show up at school. He wanted to have a new attitude, one that would bring a smile to others' faces and make him a joy to be around. He even began to think about how he could be a better leader for his teammates, knowing that was also the identity of winning teams.

He reached back over to his nightstand, grabbed his notebook once again, and opened it back up. Things were starting to click for Jai. He realized in that moment that if he wanted to win every day, he would need to treat his days differently. His habits, routines, and preparation were all about how he approached them. He wrote:

THE WINNER'S APPROACH

"That's it!" Jai had a light bulb moment and he couldn't wait to share it with Coach Victor the next day.

A Winner's Approach

NINE
CHAMPIONSHIP HABITS

Coach Victor had been noticing a shift in Jai's mindset as well. After a few days of consistent leadership from Jai in practice, Coach pulled Jai aside and handed him a dry erase marker.

"Jai," Coach Victor said as he extended his arm, marker in hand. "Go over to the whiteboard and write 'Championship Habits' on it."

Jai walked confidently up to the board and wrote the words in big, bold letters.

As he looked back at Coach Victor for affirmation, Coach nodded. "That's the next level you're ready for."

Jai smiled, though curiosity flickered across his face. "What do you mean?"

Coach Victor took the marker from Jai's hand and underlined the word "habits."

"You have all the talent in the world, Jai," Coach said. "But your habits will be what keep you successful once you attain success."

Jai listened as Coach pointed to the underlined word. Anyone can win once," he said. "But habits make it last. This is why you need to build championship habits."

———

Championship habits are the small, intentional actions repeated with discipline and purpose that separate good from great. They are the daily decisions to show up with focus, to train with urgency, to communicate with clarity, and to compete with consistency, no matter if anyone is watching or not.

These habits aren't based on your motivation or mood of the day. They are forged in preparation and measured by the standard you hold yourself to when pressure hits. Championship habits turn potential into performance and talent into trust.

They don't guarantee a trophy, but they make you worthy of one.

———

Coach turned the board and wrote another quote. He read the quote aloud:

"Under pressure, we don't rise to the occasion; we fall to the level of our training."

Coach looked at Jai and said, "It's time for you to lead by example. I want you to take this to heart and bring your teammates with you. Be the model of consistency. Show them how habits are built, day by day. When the whole team buys in, everyone grows. Think to yourself, how will you create real accountability among your teammates? The smallest details have the largest consequences."

Jai was beginning to comprehend this philosophy more and more each day. He attributed a lot of his understanding to his commitment to journaling. That night, Jai was back at his desk. It was becoming a familiar place for him as he reflected on his day, but tonight was different. Tonight he wasn't reflecting; he was planning. He flipped to the next blank page and wrote down a list of habits that win.

- **Get up early**
- **Show up on time and with the Winner's Approach**
- **Control what I can**
- **Give energy and effort that elevates everyone**
- **Have a great attitude**

He was no longer consumed by the spotlight or highlight reels. Jai was determined to build championship habits that would lead him through adversity and discomfort. Habits that would prepare him for the big moments. He knew he needed to develop processes and systems to keep him in line. He wrote:

"STACK ONE HABIT . . . ONE CHAMPIONSHIP HABIT AT A TIME."

"IF I CAN DO THIS EVERY DAY AND WIN THE MOMENT, THE SKY IS THE LIMIT."

Jai began thinking about how to hold his teammates accountable and how to invite them to do the same for him. He had a few ideas, though he wasn't sure which one was right. But he knew one thing: it didn't have to be perfect. He just had to start.

Coach Victor reminded them often:

"Little by little, a little becomes a lot. Championship habits are small . . . until they no longer are."

TEN

IDENTITY → ACTIONS → FEELINGS

ater in the week, Coach Victor called a classroom session for the team. These meetings were vital. They were times when the coaching staff would dig into the leadership principles that changed lives far beyond the court.

He wrote three words on the board.

Feelings → Actions → Identity

or

Identity → Actions → Feelings

"Which one resembles you?" Coach Victor prompted the entire team, especially Jai, to think on this. "Most people get this backward. They approach their circumstances with their feelings. 'I don't feel like practicing.' 'I don't like what just happened to me. I'm upset, so I'll check out mentally.' If you let your feelings dictate your actions, not only will you lose a lot of games, but you will lose in life too."

Coach turned back to the board and drew several circles around the word *identity*.

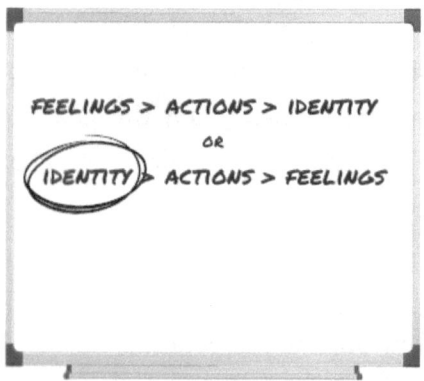

"Winners start here," he said. "They know who they are and they act on their identity. When your life is anchored in purpose, your feelings will no longer run the show, but they will follow the actions of your calling."

Coach Victor locked eyes with Jai and pointed at him. "Do you feel like you're beginning to live this out? Are you stepping into your true identity?"

Jai cracked a big smile. "Yeah, Coach. I think I am."

Jai wasn't fully sure, but he knew there was a change going on in his mindset and heartset.

"Good." Coach grinned and gave a little chuckle. "Because if your feelings are leading you, you will never have the future you desire. But if you lead in your identity, those championship habits will build you a life you never could have imagined."

Not only was Jai seeing this mindset pay off in games, but he was seeing its effects off the court too.

He now tried to approach everything he did with an elite mindset. He was more focused in class and spoke to his teachers with more respect. He was intentional in his relationships and spent more time investing in others.

People noticed he was a changed person. Not just because his game had improved, but because he was making the people around him better. His leadership was multiplying, which was a true testimony of significance.

Jai scribbled in his notebook:

A LEGACY ISN'T WHAT YOU BUILD,
IT'S WHO YOU BUILD.

Jai was starting to understand that living with championship habits didn't just elevate performance, but it also elevated leadership. It wasn't about stat sheets or game outcomes anymore. His growth was rooted in a heartset that couldn't be measured. He was beginning to live a life of purpose, on purpose.

ELEVEN
THE HEART OF THE MATTER

That same evening, Coach Victor was at his house reflecting on how he could make the greatest impact on his team. He truly wanted to see his players become better men. Coach Victor was well aware that the culture of high school and college basketball had shifted in the wrong direction. Too many coaches and leaders were more concerned with transactions over transformation. They were more focused on what a kid could do for them than how they could help the kid. That was everything Coach Victor stood against.

Wins and losses were a part of the profession, but the game was about far more than the scoreboard.

Coach Victor was committed to transforming lives, not just using players for their performance. He understood that the words he spoke to his team would eventually become the words they repeated to themselves. He took a pen and a napkin from the kitchen table and wrote down,

TRANSFORMATIONAL, NOT TRANSACTIONAL.

The phrase grounded him. It reminded him that this life, and this work, was bigger than basketball. As a fierce competitor, Coach Victor knew he needed to stay rooted in his true purpose. Especially with all of the teaching he'd been doing about *Win One Won*, he knew some might misunderstand the message. Winning was fun and good, but he wanted his team to do it for the right reasons and a bigger purpose.

He quietly asked himself, *"What kind of coach do I truly want to become?"*

"If I truly want to be a transformational coach, I need to use the game of basketball to build people up. To create leaders, not just players. I need to coach their hearts. I need to create an environment to succeed."

Coach Victor turned his attention back to the napkin and began to write. He knew he needed to stay anchored in the things that truly mattered.

He thought, *"You're not just teaching basketball. You're shaping future husbands, fathers, and leaders. Men who will serve their communities and be lights in the darkness."*

To expound on his mindset of being a transformational coach he wrote:

- CELEBRATE THE THINGS THAT ACTUALLY LEAD TO WINNING
- BUILD TRUST IN THE QUIET MOMENTS.
- THE SCORE WON'T BE REMEMBERED, BUT THEY'LL NEVER FORGET HOW YOU MADE THEM FEEL.

For Coach Victor, success was always about more than the scoreboard. His value wasn't dictated by his qualifications, record, or his passion, but by the way he consistently impacted the people under his leadership.

While Coach Victor believed in striving to win every moment, every day, he also knew that coaches needed to ensure everything they said and did was intentional. On purpose, with purpose. He needed to speak the truth in love, and do that over and over again.

TWELVE
LOCKED IN

The next day was gameday. Coach Victor gathered the team in the locker room before warm-ups. He handed the floor to the team captain, Jai.

"I know we've been talking a lot about winning," Jai began, "but last night it really hit me. Winning isn't just about the scoreboard. It's not about the points I score or the plays we run. It's about who we are every day. Coach has taught me that. It's about our approach. It's about the championship habits we build that keep us focused, locked in, and consistent."

He held up his notebook. "I've been writing it all down. And I've realized something. I haven't always showed up the right way. I've been relying on talent instead of preparation. I've been treating some games like they matter less. But Coach was right—every moment matters. Every possession matters. Every game matters."

Jai paused, his voice steady. "And if I want to be great, if *we* want to be great, we need to stop waiting for things to click. We need to decide, right now, to lock in. To win every moment, every day."

The room was quiet. For the first time all season, every single player was fully dialed in.

Coach Victor watched silently from the side of the room, pride swelling in his chest. Jai was stepping into leadership, just as he'd hoped he would.

MINDSET: WIN

WIN Mindset

Winning every moment doesn't happen by accident—it's intentional. It's built on a foundation of the Winner's Approach and Championship Habits. So how do you train yourself to win every moment, every day?

———

W – Winner's Approach

How you show up matters. Long before tipoff or applause, your approach will already establish your trajectory.

Ask yourself:

- **Am I focused or distracted?**
- **Am I early, prepared, and engaged?**
- **Am I bringing energy that elevates the room?**

The Winner's Approach is all about controlling the controllables. Your **attitude, energy, effort, and focus.**

These things require zero talent. They demand one thing: a daily decision to choose them on purpose. If you want to win the moment, you must be in the moment.

———

I – Invest in Championship Habits

When the game is on the line, you can't just snap your fingers and magically perform better. You can't rely on emotions or motivational momentum. You need to establish consistent processes and systems.

Ask yourself:

- **What routines help me stay ready even when I don't feel ready?**
- **Are my actions aligned with my goals?**
- **What distractions do I need to remove to level up?**

Remember, little by little, a little becomes a lot. Small habits compound, and when you stack days, you win more consistently.

———

N – Navigate with Intentionality

Winning doesn't happen by accident. It's intentionally engineered and designed with a purpose. Your preparation will separate you from the competition, especially when you fuel your actions in your identity.

Ask yourself:

- **Who am I when adversity hits?**
- **Do I lead with identity or react from emotion?**
- **Do I respond with purpose or impulsively check out?**

These are the true separators. High performers don't let feelings dictate their direction. They anchor to who they are. They lead with intentionality, in the dark, in the quiet, in every moment.

PART THREE
ONE
ONE REP, ONE DAY AT A TIME

THIRTEEN
I'VE GOT YOUR SIX

The week before, Coach Victor had challenged Jai to not only level up his own habits, but to raise the bar for the entire team by creating real accountability. It wasn't just a meaningless challenge. It stuck with Jai. Every time he opened his journal, the thought circled in his mind: *How do we make this special? How do we live it?*

The breakthrough came when Jai remembered a powerful school assembly years earlier. A U.S. Army veteran had spoken about what it meant to truly have someone's back on the battlefield and in life.

The soldier called it "having your six."

———

In military terms, your "six" refers to anything behind you, like on a clock face. It was your blindspot. In combat, watching each other's six isn't optional; it's life or death. There's a blind trust and it's non-negotiable. You don't just watch out for yourself, you protect the person next to you, and they do the same.

The veteran shared that no matter how skilled or disciplined you are, everyone has blind spots. And if you're relying only on your own awareness to survive, you're vulnerable. Real strength comes when people around you are committed to seeing what you can't and calling it out before it's too late.

———

That message struck a chord with Jai.

What if his team operated that way? What if they weren't just teammates, but accountability partners—six partners? Jai proposed the idea the next day that every player would be paired with someone else. Their job? Watch each other's six. Challenge, encourage, and hold each other to the team's standard, both on and off the court.

At first, the team loved it. The energy changed and they began checking in with each other, reminding each other of habits and goals.

But soon, the reality of accountability set in.

It was easy to call someone else out. It was much harder to *be* called out. Everyone likes being the standard until someone holds the mirror up.

Jai found himself in a tough spot. He had introduced the concept, but now he had to live it.

He was slipping. His attitude had taken a hit. He was dwelling on mistakes too long, and it showed. The team noticed. So did Coach Victor. In one practice, frustration boiled over. Jai missed a free throw, proceeded to give up an easy lay-up, and dropped a cuss word in anger, breaking Coach Victor's well-known team rule: *no cussing.*

His teammates didn't let it slide. "That's not what we do, Jai," one of them said, firm but respectful.

Instead of owning it, Jai snapped.

"Dude, leave me alone. I never should've come up with this six-partner thing. You guys don't understand the pressure I'm under. Just let me be me."

The gym went quiet.

Coach Victor watched, but he wasn't angry. He saw the internal battle playing out in Jai. He didn't rush to fix it. He knew this was part of it.

The team was learning something deeper than discipline or strategy. They were learning that accountability isn't just about correcting others, it's about *inviting correction*. It's about choosing growth over comfort. And for leaders like Jai, it means giving others permission to challenge you, even when it stings.

That day, Jai wasn't ready to receive it. But Coach Victor knew he eventually would.

The idea of "having your six" wasn't just a catchy phrase anymore. It was becoming a foundational piece of the team.

And though Jai was wrestling with the weight of leadership, he knew he needed iron sharpening iron. The team didn't need a perfect leader. They needed an *authentic* one. And if Jai stayed in the fight, he would become just that.

But at that moment, the pressure was getting to him. His reactions and emotions bled into practice, and they would follow him into the next game.

FOURTEEN
NEXT PLAY MENTALITY

"Next play!" Coach Victor screamed from the sidelines, his voice reverberating off the gym walls. "Next play mentality!" The team was struggling and down by ten when they committed another unforced turnover, their third in the last four possessions. Coach was frustrated. The players were frustrated. It wasn't just the mistakes, it was the momentum they kept surrendering. Yet they were trained in moving on from mistakes and not allowing them to affect the next play.

At first, the "next-play mentality" didn't make sense to Jai. He and his teammates used to roll their eyes when Coach kept repeating "next play" after every error.

Jai would have thoughts such as, *Coach just needs to let me express my frustration* or *I'm only mad because I expect better from myself. It's passion.*

While there might be some truth to those thoughts, Jai didn't understand how holding on to the past was affecting his future. He hadn't yet realized that moving on to the next play and forgetting about what just happened would be a catalyst for success in his life for years to come.

He had spent so much time focused on the "Win" aspect of *Win One Won* and growing in winning every moment every day. But now, it was time to grow again.

During this game, Jai began to truly understand what it meant to move on. He began to understand the power of persisting through obstacles and difficulty, one possession at a time, even when things weren't going his way.

One moment in particular really made an impact on Jai. In the past, anytime he or any of his teammates made a mistake, they would immediately be subbed out of the game. Jai always felt this destroyed his confidence and fueled his frustration. Late in the fourth quarter, with the game on the line, Jai found himself in a similar situation. In a moment when his team couldn't afford to make a mistake, Jai dribbled the ball off his foot. He couldn't believe it. You could feel the tension in the gym, and Jai had a sinking feeling in his stomach. He was ready to be subbed out.

As Jai looked to the bench expecting to see a new player at the scorer's table, he instead saw Coach Victor clapping and encouraging him to move on to the "next play!"

Jai was stunned but instantly snapped back into action.

On the very next possession, he sprinted back, took a charge, and the entire building erupted! They got the ball back and scored to extend their lead. A shift happened when Jai moved on to the next play. Not only in the game, but in his mindset.

Despite the team's struggles and constant mistakes, he learned to take comfort in the wisdom coming from the bench. "Next play!"

He could see in his teammates' eyes that they believed. Even after another turnover, they were determined to respond. Nobody hung their heads. Nobody jogged back on defense. Instead, all five players sprinted back and stayed locked in for the next possession. Their communication was on point, and they kept playing with energy no matter what had just gone wrong.

The momentum shifted. The energy was elevated.

And guess what?

They won the game.

That's the power of the Next Play.

FIFTEEN
REACT VS. RESPOND

The next-play mentality is a mindset that can change the trajectory of your future. It matters, and it's something that every leader needs to adapt into their toolkit.

The day after their previous game, Coach Victor dedicated the entire film session to this principle. As he stood quietly in front of the room, he wrote three words on the whiteboard:

REACT – RESET – RESPOND

"We will never be perfect." Coach Victor was ready to elaborate. "We can strive for perfection, but we will never reach it. Mistakes are going to happen. It's inevitable. But if we are prepared for these moments, we can move on quickly and efficiently.

"Last night I saw a team that wanted to win. I saw your heart and desire, but I also saw hesitation."

Coach Victor pointed to the board. "This is what we are talking about today. Not X's and O's. Not missed box-outs or missed switches.

This."

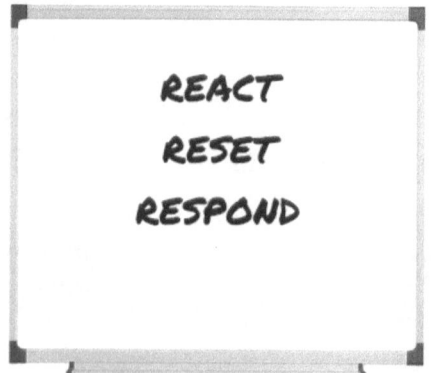

He underlined the first word.

REACT.

"This is our natural instinct as humans. When things happen to us in life, we all have emotions and will react accordingly. But leaders don't stay here. They develop the ability to recognize it and shift their focus to something more profitable."

Many of the players shifted around in their seats as they thought about their negative reactions the night before.

"We need to understand and control our reaction time. The quicker we can move on from a mistake, the better we can be for our teammates and the ultimate outcome," Coach Victor said.

He moved on to the next word.

RESET.

"Take a deep breath. Stay in control of your reaction and take a moment to clear your mind."

Coach Victor looked around the room and locked eyes with every player.

"Momentum lives in the present. Last night, we had moments where momentum was ours to take, but we stayed stuck in what just happened. Once you decided to reset your mind, you were able to move on to the next phase, which is our response."

RESPOND.

"This is where champions live—in the response. They train their minds and their hearts to be prepared for every situation possible. When that time comes, they limit their reaction time, reset quickly, and respond with intention and purpose."

He stepped away from the board and gave a final message to the team.

"We aren't trying to be perfect, but we are trying to be prepared for the battles we will face. When the pressure rises, we need to be able to rely on our training and respond to any circumstance."

The room was quiet and the players in the room had clarity.

Coach finished by saying, "If you want to win the moments, you've got to master the details. This starts with how you respond. Responses are intentional and they're fully in your control."

Jai was beginning to internalize Coach's teachings. For his entire high school career, Jai had thought he needed to be perfect. He knew he wasn't, but he always felt the pressure to perform without making mistakes. What he was realizing, though, was that perfection is a lie, and mistakes are inevitable. No matter if you're an athlete, a coach, or an entrepreneur, leaders mess up. He was realizing that his goal shouldn't be to avoid mistakes, but to respond and avoid allowing one mistake to become two. Once Jai let go of the need to be perfect, he started to see the game, and life, differently.

———

Whether you're playing in a basketball game or living your everyday life, it's happening in real time. Anytime you take your focus off of what's next, you slow yourself down. Momentum lives in the present and the best performers protect it. A quick reset gives them the competitive edge. They harness the power that the next-play mentality brings.

In fact, our response is one of the most important things we will ever have as leaders. Anyone can lead when it's easy. But optimal performers know that true grit and real belief is forged when things go wrong. You can either react to the circumstance, or you can respond. The choice is yours.

Jai was learning this lesson on the fly and was trying his best to become a leader who responds rather than reacts.

You see, when we react we lose control. We are making decisions based on feelings, and there is no premeditated response to failure. Reactions are impulsive and they often spiral before we have a chance to adjust.

Responses, on the other hand, are planned for. There is intentionality to what we will do next after a mistake happens. We've seen it happen in our mind before and we are prepared to respond, which generates an action that is under control. This is where we need to grow if we want to fully embody the next-play mentality.

———

Ever since Jai had seen how the next-play mentality changed his mindset and gave him confidence to keep performing at a high level, he'd been locked in.

This mindset shift helped Jai turn his post-mistake reactions into intentional responses. He used to think the next-play mentality only mattered if the last play was good. But now he knew the next play matters most when the last one wasn't.

SIXTEEN
FLIP THE SCRIPT

The following week of practice felt off. One day in particular everything seemed to be going awry. The team lacked focus. Missed layups, sloppy turnovers, poor body language. They were coming off a gritty win, but there seemed to be something weighing on everyone beyond basketball.

Coach Victor could tell something deeper was going on. After another missed layup, he blew his whistle. "Bring it in." The players could tell he was frustrated, but they also sensed Coach's genuine concern.

As the players huddled up, sweaty and unfocused, Coach Victor paused. Surveying the room, he looked around and turned his attention to Jai.

"What's going on out here today?"

Jai struggled to make eye contact and shrugged his shoulders. "I don't know, Coach. Nothing seems to be clicking today. We're off as a team."

Coach Victor nodded in agreement. After getting input from some of the other guys, he said, "Yeah, I agree. And do you know why?"

The team stood there, still lacking clarity.

"Because you are letting your feelings dictate your actions. That's not leadership."

Now that Coach had everyone's attention, he took a deep breath and leaned into his guys.

"This isn't anything I haven't seen before." Coach Victor had the focus of everyone. "You miss a couple shots and your body language suffers. You get held accountable by a teammate and you check out mentally. Fatigue sets in and you stop sprinting down the floor. If your feelings drive your behavior, your performance will always suffer."

Coach Victor paused and let his words sink in a little more.

"If you continue to live this way, you're in danger of losing more than just a game."

Jai could feel the truth of these words, and it hit him hard. He knew deep down that he was guilty of allowing his feelings to dictate his actions. And not just today, but a lot of days before.

Coach took a deep breath and got real with the team.

"I'm going to tell you something that I haven't shared with you before."

Everyone was locked in as Coach began.

"When I was your age, I battled some health issues and struggled with my purpose. I loved the game of basketball and I was pretty good at it. But when that love was taken away from me, I didn't know how to handle it. I became bitter and angry at the world, and no one was safe from my sour attitude. I no longer had a sense of identity because my identity had always been wrapped up in what I could do on the basketball court."

The gym was silent.

"Then one day I had a coach pull me aside and tell me something that would change my life forever. He said, 'You're living life backward. You are allowing your feelings to lead your actions, and it's stealing your joy. You need to flip it before your identity crumbles.'"

Coach Victor grabbed the dry erase board sitting on the scorer's table and wrote down three familiar words. "We talked about this a few weeks ago; do you remember?"

IDENTITY → ACTIONS → FEELINGS

"This became a heartset for my life. I no longer allowed my confidence to come from how I felt that day. I came to know Jesus as my Savior and found my identity as a child of God. I knew who I was, and I chose to base my actions on my identity, not my feelings. Ironically, by doing so, my feelings became happier and more joyful."

After practice, Jai decided to stick around for a little while and have a conversation with Coach Victor.

"Coach," Jai began, "how did you figure out what your identity was?"

Coach Victor smiled. "Prayer. Life throws a lot at you. When I put my faith and trust in Jesus, I knew that no matter what happened to me, He was in control. Purpose made the pressure feel smaller. I saw my life was bigger than basketball."

He continued, "I know you're more than a basketball player too, Jai. When you begin to step into your identity and your true calling, you will begin to lean into the leader you were meant to be. Take some time to journal about that this week."

That night, Jai went home and began to journal. He opened his notebook and wrote at the top of the page, "My identity is greater than what I do. Who am I?"

> *My identity is bigger than what I do.*
>
> *Who am I?*

He began to write a few bullet points:

- **I am a child of God.**
- **I am a leader.**
- **I am consistent.**
- **I respond, not react.**

Jai closed his eyes and said to himself, *"Even when I don't feel like it, I'm going lean into who I was created to be. I know this is all bigger than the game of basketball."*

———

Identity

Who *are* you every day, even when things get hard? Define it and write it down. Strive to be this person consistently . . . every day. Live it.

Actions

When you are living in your identity, what would you do right now? How would you lead with character? How would you show up for those around you?

Feelings

Your fulfillment will come from aligning with your identity. Confidence and joy grow from daily consistency. Choose joy.

As the team rallied around this new heartset, they began to play better. Not because they stopped making mistakes, but because they bounced back quicker. They were mentally ready because they knew who they were both as individuals and as a team.

SEVENTEEN
FORGED THROUGH FIRE

Adversity was normal for Coach Victor throughout his whole life. He never had it easy, and he didn't always respond well.

Adversity is often misrepresented as something that only affects the mind, but Coach Victor had learned it could weigh heavily on the heart as well.

Coach Victor had to learn this the hard way, which was a big reason why he wanted to help the next generation. He found out that the way we face challenges has more to do with the condition of our heart attitude than the circumstances around us. In order for us to grow and overcome adversity, we need to get our heart right in humility, commitment, and resilience.

When we are squeezed, adversity simply reveals whatever is already inside of us. We could be holding on to anger, bitterness, pride, or fear, but whatever is inside our hearts is going to spill out. Coach Victor had to train his mind and shape his heart to make sure he overcame adversity one day at a time.

Coach Victor was born with a rare disease that limited him in so many ways. He wanted to be the best and compete at a high level, but unfortunately he was unable to achieve many of his dreams through athletics. He vividly remembered a conversation he'd had with God when he was a teenager.

"God, why are you doing this to me? You know I love sports and I am good at them. I hate that you're putting me through this, and it's really angering me. Clearly, you don't have my best interest in mind."

That prayer revealed just how much bitterness he's been holding and how much it was already costing him.

His life changed when he met a couple coaches who poured into him and showed him how to shift his responses to a more productive outcome.

"Why me?" Leads to frustration and keep you stuck in the past.

"I'm not good enough" breeds shame and fear, crippling any chance you had of being great.

"Nobody understands me" fills you with pride and keeps you from grasping the lessons all around you.

These coaches helped Coach Victor see a better way. They showed him how his pride and bitterness created walls and shut people out. They gave him wisdom and directed him to think with humility and grace. He didn't realize it at the time, but this simple mindset and heartset shift would be something that would change his life.

———

Jai had shown a lot of growth, but was still struggling to be consistent in many leadership areas. The adversity in his life had proved to be overwhelming more often than not, and sometimes he questioned if he would ever grasp everything Coach Victor had been trying to teach him. He wondered if he was the only one who battled these things in his mind, or if others encountered the same things as he did.

His last high school game was quickly approaching, and Jai wished he felt better about his progress than he did. He was searching for answers and wanted it to all make sense in that moment.

So when Jai wrapped up his high school career and opened a handwritten note from Coach Victor before Senior Night, it was refreshing to know he wasn't alone. It read:

"JAI, IT'S BEEN A TRUE JOY COACHING YOU. YOU'VE GROWN SO MUCH AND STILL HAVE SO MUCH MORE TO GIVE. ALWAYS REMEMBER THAT THE HEART OF THE MATTER IS A MATTER OF THE HEART. WHEN YOU HURT, LEARN FROM IT, AND YOU WILL BE UNSTOPPABLE. GOD HAS BIG THINGS IN STORE FOR YOU AS YOU MOVE ON TO COLLEGE, BUT NEVER FORGET THAT IT DOESN'T MATTER WHAT HAPPENS TO YOU, IT'S WHAT HAPPENS THROUGH YOU."

That night, Jai played the best game of his career because he knew he could play free. Coach Victor had shown him how to win the moment, one day at a time. He knew if he approached his last game with the Winner's Approach and carried over his championship habits, nothing could stand in his way. He had prepared for adversity and trusted he would respond with the next-play mentality if and when it struck. He was ready for the moment in both his heart and his mind. He knew the adventure wasn't over, but he was finding joy in the process.

As Jai sat on the bench soaking in the culmination of his high school career, he saw Coach Victor give a subtle nod to a man patiently waiting in the corner of the gym. At first, Jai didn't recognize this man, but as he approached, he could tell it was the coach from his dream college.

"Great game! My name is Coach Ellis. I've been watching you for a while. Not just your game, but more importantly how you carry yourself. The way you compete. I love it!"

Jai was surprised to hear this feedback. "Thanks, Coach. It means a lot that you came out to the game tonight."

"Listen, I don't know if you know this, but I played for Coach Victor, and when he took the job here, he told me I needed to keep an eye on you. He's filled me in on your growth, and I want to see if it can translate to the next level. I know you'd thrive in our culture, and I think we can do something special. I have one scholarship left, and it's yours if you want it."

Jai took a deep breath and couldn't believe this had just happened. He instantly connected with Coach Ellis and wondered if this was the place for him. He was anticipating what was next.

From across the gym, Coach Victor watched the handshake between Jai and Coach Ellis. He didn't say much, but the smile on his face said everything. He was proud. Not because Jai earned a scholarship, but because Jai had become the kind of young man who was ready for it. This was the moment he'd been working toward all season. Not the offer itself, but the growth that made it possible.

EIGHTEEN
CALLED UP

While getting a full-ride offer to play college basketball was a dream come true for Jai, a new wave of anxiety crept into his mind. From the outside, Jai looked confident as his high school career ended on a high. But inside, doubt was louder than ever. He felt like an imposter.

The more he thought about committing to Coach Ellis, the more Jai began to wonder if he was good enough to compete at the next level.

He was fighting an internal battle.

"What if I can't perform in college?"

"Do I really deserve this?"

"What if they find out I'm not who they think I am?"

These questions ate away at Jai. He felt like a fraud.

Determined to prove he belonged, he spent hours upon hours in the gym trying to perfect his craft. He was obsessed, driven not by hunger, but by fear. He placed an immense amount of pressure on himself to perform at a high level and wouldn't let himself stop until it was perfect.

But the more he pressed, the worse he felt. His mind was off. His confidence was shaken. He was completely lost.

Wanting to push himself harder, Jai invited one of his teammates to join him for a workout. Zion, known to everyone on the team as "Z," was Jai's go-to guy. Z wasn't just a teammate, he was Jai's "six partner," the one who had his back on and off the court. But as they got into the session, Z noticed something was off. Jai was attacking every drill with reckless intensity, overdoing every rep like he had something to prove.

As the workout progressed, both Jai and Z were exhausted. Neither of them were enjoying it. The workout was no longer productive, just punishing.

Finally, Z called him out.

"What's going on, man?" he asked. "You just got an offer to play at your dream school, but you're working out like you're angry. Why?"

Jai shrugged it off. "This is what the best players do." he insisted. "I've seen it. They workout for hours upon hours and it's the only way to get better. Everyone expects me to be great at the next level, so this is what I gotta do."

Z didn't buy it.

"I get it. You want to be the best. But today you weren't just working hard, you were running from something. What's up?"

"Don't worry about it." Jai snapped, grabbing the ball from his teammates hands. "If you don't want to push yourself this hard, you can just leave. I don't need you here."

Z didn't budge and followed him. "Hold up, Jai," he said in a calm, but firm voice. "I'm not letting you carry this by yourself. Talk to me. I know you. This isn't just about basketball. What's *really* going on?"

Jai couldn't look up and was on the verge of tears. He tried to act tough, but it didn't work. The pressure finally cracked through and he broke down.

"I'm afraid I'm not going to be good enough." Jai was peeling back the fear inside his heart. "I should be enjoying this offer, but all I feel is fear. Fear of letting people down. Fear of falling short of the expectations. I feel . . . lost."

This is why "six partners" mattered. It's not just about calling someone out, it's about *calling them up*. Z understood it was time to speak truth over his lies.

"Do you remember that day Coach Victor stopped practice to talk to us about our identity?" he asked. "What do you believe about yourself right now? Are you leading from your identity, or from the lies the enemy is feeding you?

Jai took a deep breath and wiped away the tears that were streaming down his cheeks.

"I don't know, man. I thought I knew who I was, but I. . . I don't know. I feel like I have no clue who I am."

"I'm here for you, Jai," Z said as he began to speak life into Jai. "You've told us who you are. You're a leader. You're consistent. But most of all, you're a Child of God. I've been there too, man. I've listened to the lies, but I've learned that fear is a liar. The truth? You are good enough and you're called to this."

Jai appreciated the words from his teammate, but was still struggling with getting his mind out of this dark place. Z knew this and gave him one more reminder.

"It's time to respond, Jai. You've been our rock all year, but now *I've* got your six. Next play."

A small smile broke across Jai's face. "You sound like Coach Victor."

Z laughed. "Nah. I sound like *you*."

They dapped each other up and began to head out of the gym. But Jai paused and began jogging back out to the court.

"Gotta end on a make bro."

They both knocked down one more shot and walked off the floor. They knew who they were.

Their identity wasn't rooted in performance or pressure. It was rooted in purpose. The lies had no place left to hide.

Accountability matters. Having someone who will tell you the truth, fight for your identity, and call you up instead of out.

That's how growth happens. This is the power of the brotherhood.

MINDSET: ONE

ONE Mindset

Resetting quickly after setbacks is a competitive advantage. We know our approach and habits allow us to win each moment, but to reach our potential, we need a repeatable system we can execute daily.

O – Own the Moment

Have you ever been in the room, but not really in the moment? This mindset doesn't lead to much.

Winners don't drift. They own the moment. This means accepting responsibility for your actions, locking in on what's in front of you, and eliminating excuses without blame, comparison, or distraction.

Ask yourself:

- **What does this moment need from me?**
- **Am I focused on what I can control or am I distracted?**
- **Am I reacting or responding?**

———

N – Next-Play Mentality

Whether you just made a mistake or the best play of your career, successful leaders don't stay there. They move on to the next play, and do so quickly.

Winners control their actions. Reacting is emotional. Responding is intentional. Great leaders move on with clarity, letting go of failure without losing confidence, and letting go of success without losing focus. It's not about forgetting what happened, but it's about intentionally shaping what comes next.

Ask yourself:

- What can I learn from the moment that just happened?
- What things do I need to let go of so I can move forward?
- What is the next best action I can take?

Recognize your emotions in the moment. Reset your focus and body language. Respond with intention and purpose.

That's how leaders move.

———

E – Execute in Your Identity

It's not just about getting the job done and moving on, but it's about doing it by knowing your greater purpose. When you know who you are, you never sacrifice what you want most for what you want in the moment. Instead, your actions will flow directly from your identity and allow you to move on quickly with composure and clarity. This is where consistency becomes anchored. When identity leads, confidence follows.

Ask yourself:

- Who am I? Who am I becoming?
- Who do I have in my life holding me accountable? Am I doing the same for others in my life?
- Am I acting from my calling or from my feelings?

Compete with joy. Compete with purpose. Move on to the next play, quickly.

PART FOUR
WON
AT THE END OF THE DAY, YOU'LL HAVE WON

NINETEEN
WHAT COMES NEXT

While Jai didn't need long to decide on his college future, he was just now beginning to step into his true identity as a leader. His teammate called him up to something greater and now he just needed to talk to Coach Victor about the next steps.

Jai's confidence was rising, not because of the offer or his success on the basketball court, but because of the growth he had earned by embracing the *Win One Won* philosophy.

There was no doubt he had learned how to show up with the Winner's Approach more consistently. He'd changed the way he walked into a room and immediately understood how his presence could change the mood of everyone around him.

He knew that energy elevates and that his attitude and body language communicated to everyone how he was going to act that day. After all, body language doesn't whisper—it screams! Jai had become someone who dictated the temperature of the room, a thermostat, not a thermometer. He was a tone setter for everyone else around him. He had put in the time to build championship habits with intentional consistency. Jai knew he was ready for the next phase of his career.

"I know I have a long way to go and have a lot to learn, but I'm extremely grateful for the growth I've made in just a couple short years with you, Coach," Jai said. "Coach Ellis seems like a great guy, and the fact that he played for you makes me believe he will continue teaching me the same lessons you've taught me. Do you think I should go play for him?"

"I will tell you this, Jai. I've never seen a player embrace the idea of *Win One Won* as much as you have. I believe you've put yourself in a great position to be successful because of your buy-in to this. In fact, you remind me a lot of Coach Ellis when he was a player."

"Do you remember our first meeting when I told you about the former player of mine who went on this *Win One Won* journey with me?" Coach Victor asked. "Well, that was

Coach Ellis. He was the best there was, but he lacked something deeper. At that point in my career I was learning for myself how to win every moment, every day, and Coach Ellis was able to go on that adventure with me. He grew right alongside me, and I've been able to see him take this philosophy and framework further than I ever could have. I actually have watched him implement the *Won* part of this better than anyone, and he's helped me grow as a human being and a leader."

"Wow. That's really cool to hear, Coach. It's always been my dream to play at that college, and ever since Coach Ellis arrived, they've made it to the tournament every season. I would love to make it to the Final Four and win a national championship." Jai was daydreaming of what that moment would look like. "Do you think that's possible?"

Coach Victor grinned. "Jai, I think you're the type of player Coach Ellis has been waiting for. He has built a culture of success, and it wasn't by accident. If he has the players in his program who know and truly believe they can win every moment, every day, the sky is the limit. And guess what, I believe you're that type of player."

Jai couldn't believe what he was hearing. Ever since he was a little boy he had dreamed of playing at the next level, the highest level. And now it was all coming to fruition right before his eyes. The offer was on the table, his coach supported him, and he felt ready to make a decision.

"Coach," Jai began , "can we call Coach Ellis together and give him the good news? I want to make this official."

"Of course we can, Jai. You just tell me when."

TWENTY
LEVELING UP

The next morning, Coach Ellis woke up and was preparing his mind and body for the day. He had fine-tuned his morning routine for years and rarely veered from it. Before his feet even touched the floor, he said a prayer of gratitude for another day and asked God for wisdom to lead properly in any situation thrown at him that day. He ate a healthy breakfast, hydrated, and worked out. It was nothing too crazy, but he had learned to be consistent in his routine. After all, he had a lot of experience with *Win One Won* and knew how important a Winner's Approach for creating championship habits.

As he was finishing up his morning prep, his phone rang. It put an instant smile on his face when he saw the caller ID was from "Coach Victor."

"Coach! So good to hear from you. How are you doing? Anything I can do for you?" Coach Ellis was genuinely joyful to get this call from his friend, mentor, and old ball coach.

"Well, I'm glad I could put a smile on your face today. I actually have someone with me right now who can't wait to speak with you. I'm going to hand the phone over to him." Coach Victor passed the phone to Jai so he could tell Coach Ellis the good news.

"Coach Ellis, this is Jai. I hope you're doing well. When you gave me an offer the other day, I instantly felt a connection with you. I could tell you were a genuine person, and I've seen the success you've had with your teams. I spent a lot of time in prayer and discussing this decision with my family and with Coach Victor. I wanted to let you know I would be grateful and humbled to accept your offer to come play for you at the next level."

"Let's go! I love to hear this, Jai. I've been praying that God would bring the right people into our program, and I think you're just the guy. This is the best news I've received in a long time! I'm pumped."

When Coach Ellis spoke about the "right people," he was referring to people who:

- Believe in, and buy into the vision and mission.
- Embody the standards of the program.
- Take ownership because they are accountable and trustworthy.
- Put the team first.
- Give everything they have.
- Want to grow and will work to achieve it.
- Enjoy the adventure while building relationships with the people they work with.

Coach Victor chimed in, "Jai has shown exceptional growth in his ability to win the moment, one day at a time. I've told him it's time to level up and learn how to sustain all the success he's going to have. I know you're the right leader who will help him instill the final part of *Win One Won*. What do you think of that?"

Coach Ellis loved what he was hearing. Jai's character stood out most. The talent and skill was just icing on the cake. But the way Jai showed up every day with the Winner's Approach and how he developed championship habits was what sealed it. Coach Ellis was honored that Coach Victor trusted him to continue leading Jai in his career.

"Wow, Coach. I'm honored that you trust me so much and

believed in me enough to recommend me to Jai," Coach Ellis said.

He turned his attention back to Jai. "And yes, I will pour into you as you continue to grow and advance in this adventure. I think you're ready to learn the concept *Won*. And by that I mean you're ready to compound your success, sustain your excellence, and grow in your significance. Are you ready to go?"

"Let's do it!" Jai exclaimed. "I am so excited to play for you, Coach. We are going to do something special."

TWENTY-ONE
THE CULTURE THAT CHANGED EVERYTHING

Coach Ellis had just led his team through the most successful season in program history. A conference championship. A national tournament run. National attention. From the outside, it looked like a dream.

But things were not always functioning properly, as Coach Ellis could attest to when he took over the job just a few years earlier. Not everyone remembered how broken things once were.

He'd inherited a team that had endured twenty-one consecutive losing seasons without ever achieving a bid to the national tournament. The morale was low, donors were lackluster in their giving, and the support from administration was nearly nonexistent. The job came with no guarantees. Just a low-budget, high-risk hire in a young coach with no college playing experience.

But Coach Ellis didn't flinch.

He took everything in stride. Because of his experience with *Win One Won*, he knew he couldn't fix all these issues in one day. Instead, it was going to be a process that required him to approach each day with grit and purpose. He was going to need to win every moment, one day at a time, and he did just that.

Little by little, things began to shift.

He put people first. He brought energy and enthusiasm back to the community. He did everything with a servant's heart and a purposeful mission.

Today, the program is unrecognizable from the one he inherited. It's not just competitive, it's respected. Players want to be there. Fans care again. The foundation is strong, and because of that, the team can now build higher than anyone once thought possible. To be where they are today is nothing short of a miracle, all thanks to the culture Coach

Ellis had built. He truly had laid a solid foundation that had allowed him to build stronger than most could have imagined.

When a leader builds on a firm foundation, they stand strong during shaky moments. That is how lasting impact is made. That is how the game is truly won. Through compounding success, sustaining excellence, and finding significance.

That's what Coach Ellis had always believed. And it's how this program moved from losing records to lasting impact.

Now, with the program's culture firmly rooted and the standard clearly defined, Coach Ellis wasn't chasing validation. He was now cultivating legacy. The goal was no longer just to win games but to develop people. And as new players stepped into the locker room, they weren't just joining a team. They were stepping into a daily pursuit of growth, purpose, and excellence. Coach Ellis knew the next chapter wasn't about maintaining success. It was about multiplying it.

TWENTY-TWO
STACKING WINS

Coach Ellis stood alone in his office, soaking in the moment. He stared at the framed photo on his wall of the team celebrating their trip to the national tournament last season. While it was a moment every coach dreams of, he knew this year's team was capable of much more. They could make a run at a national championship, but it wouldn't happen by accident.

Just a few years earlier, no one had expected anything from this program. Coaches came and their careers died. Players came and left to find something better. Championships were the furthest thing from anyone's mind. But through relentless commitment to *Win One Won*, Coach Ellis had done the impossible.

He didn't show up with flash and didn't promise instant success. But he did show up every single day. And he did so on purpose, with purpose.

This is how success compounds.

This was something Coach Victor instilled in him as a player and as a coach. Consistency wins. He had a sign hanging in his office that read, "24 x 24 x 24," which was a great reminder to stack wins and stack great days together.

$$24 \times 24 \times 24$$

Coach Ellis knew the scoreboard wouldn't change overnight. This was going to be a process amid a lot of obstacles. The players were discouraged. The community was no longer interested in what was going on at the school. After twenty-one straight losing seasons, it was amazing that anyone wanted this job in the first place.

But Coach Ellis wasn't interested in fixing the program in one day. He had a long-term vision that extended beyond anyone's immediate belief. All he was focused on was winning that day. He constantly preached the power of getting 1 percent better with every rep. He knew that little by little, a little would become a lot.

At first it was small. One more player doing an extra lift. Committing one less turnover in practice. Locking in just a little bit more on the game plan. And then something began to happen. Trust grew. The team approached every day with elite effort. Championship habits were formed. Belief began to overtake the room. As the standards rose one by one, big things began to take shape within the program.

Success isn't always fun along the adventure. It's a grind. But with the Winner's Approach and championship habits, you begin to build something others can't quite see yet.

Coach Ellis would always say, "You don't have to be amazing or perfect today. You just have to be a little better than you were yesterday. And then do it again tomorrow."

That's the secret to compounding success. Stay consistent.

Coach Ellis was ready to introduce a vision to reignite his team. Responding to their success was going to be crucial, and he didn't want to just be a one-hit wonder. If they were going to keep growing and improving on their success, they were going to have to adopt a new mindset.

After attending a coaching convention and hearing several clinics from elite coaches, Coach Ellis drew up this through process that would spark the hearts and minds of his team to compound their success.

- **Clarity** – Know what you're building. You need a vision and direction.

If you don't have purpose in your success, you'll be empty. Compounding requires direction. Who do we want to become? What kind of culture are we shaping? What matters most?

- **Consistency** – Don't get bored with the basics. Master the mundane of being an everyday person.

Showing up daily with the Winner's Approach is where growth comes from. Have the discipline to refrain from getting bored with the basics. What do we do that will reinforce who we are? Are we doing hard things even when they aren't convenient? Is our standard the same in the unseen hours as it is in the spotlight?

- **Compounding** – When you give clarity time and you trust your consistency, you will see growth and momentum.

It's not always about doing more. Breakthrough often occurs after doing what matters, long enough to make a difference. Where are we seeing growth? What small wins are we stacking every day? Where are we building momentum?

Coach Ellis knew how important it was to have a firm foundation. The culture he'd built was never about hype, and he wouldn't allow it to become about hype, even after some success. He knew culture was all about the championship habits they were creating. It was about how the team acted, interacted, and responded to everything in front of them. Players wanted to come play for him because they knew they would grow. Not just as athletes, but as men.

"CULTURE IS HOW WE:
ACT, INTERACT, AND RESPOND."

And that's why this year was going to be special. The right people were in the room, and they were locked in to do something special. It was a team built on a mindset to compound success.

"When you have a solid foundation, you don't panic when things get shaky," Coach Ellis told his team. "You don't quit when things get hard. You just keep stacking days, one day at a time."

TWENTY-THREE
SUSTAINING EXCELLENCE

The season had been going immensely well and the team morale was at an all-time high. Entering early January, the bulk of the conference season was getting underway. Jai knew this time of the year was important and was staying locked in for a strong finish. His eyes were on a much bigger prize than just going 10–0 in the non-conference season.

Practice had just ended and the gym was now quiet. The lights were dim and the sun was setting outside. Most of Jai's teammates had already left or were in the locker room hitting the showers. He was all by himself in the gym. The only sounds were the buzzing lights and ball he was bouncing. It was pure bliss and he was alone in his thoughts. In his mind, there was nowhere he'd rather be.

Coach Ellis walked in the gym with his clipboard in hand. He wanted to visualize and walk through some of the plays he'd just drawn up in his office. He loved seeing Jai in there still grinding.

"Hey," Coach called out with a smile, "how long do you need me to keep the gym open for you?"

Jai couldn't help but laugh. As he wiped the sweat from his forehead and swished another free throw, he was yearning to ask Coach Ellis something that had been on his mind for some time. "Coach, do you ever feel like . . . like everything's clicking for you? But at the same time you have this fear because it's almost too good to be true?"

Coach Ellis put his clipboard up against the wall. "That's the pressure of staying at the top. I'm right there with you, trying to navigate it myself."

Jai nodded in agreement. "I love how I'm playing right now. It's what I've always dreamed of. I'm leading well and competing at a high level. And the thing I'm most proud of is how consistent I've been with it all. But I can't shake this feeling and uncertainty of how long can I keep this up?"

Coach grabbed the ball from Jai's hands and spun it slowly for a moment. After a brief pause he said, "You've done a fantastic job of putting the work in to get to this point. But what all high performers need to understand is that excellence isn't about arriving at something. It's about enduring and sustaining it, moment after moment, day after day."

Coach Ellis passed the ball back to Jai.

"Let me ask you a question," he began. "What happens to the majority of people when they begin to experience a significant amount of success?"

After a few seconds of thought, Jai answered. "They ease up and let their guard down?"

"Exactly! For some reason, when people experience success, they get comfortable and settle. They stop doing all the things that got them there in the first place," Coach Ellis explained. "Do you think what you've done so far this season will be enough to get us all the way through March and accomplish our goals?"

"No," Jai admitted. "Everyone is going to keep getting better and better. I need to . . . *we* need to stay locked in."

"Sustaining excellence is more than pure effort and determination. It's the ability to intentionally recommit yourself to the process every single day," Coach said.

"I definitely understand that, but how do I do that?" Jai slumped against the wall in a moment of confident confusion. "How do I keep this edge about me without losing my fire?"

Coach Ellis nodded his head as if to say, "I thought you'd never ask!" even though he knew that question was going to come at some point or another.

"You've put the work in and you've learned to trust your preparation. You know how to win the moment with a winner's approach, you've established great championship habits, and now it's time to make the next shift, building systems to sustain your winning ways."

Coach Ellis noticed something poking out of Jai's backpack over by the bleachers. "Is that your same notebook from high school? The one where you track all your habits and write down your wins for the day?"

"Every day!" Jai was excited that Coach Ellis noticed. "I have been doing that for three years straight now."

Coach Ellis loved to hear that. "Love it. Keep doing that, but prepare yourself to go deeper now. You're ready. It's time to reflect more and stretch yourself to the next level. Don't just ask yourself how you did, but ask who you were in those moments. Remember, excellence isn't an outcome, it's a mindset that is constantly being renewed. If you want to be elite, you need to know how to sustain the standard of excellence.

"I'll be right back, Jai. Hang tight," Coach said.

Jai sat down on the court, legs outstretched, and began to sift through his old notes. He let his mind wander a bit, but came to the conclusion, *This makes sense. I don't have to stay hot all the time, but I need to stay consistent.*

Coach Ellis didn't take much time to run to his office and come back with a piece of paper in his hands. "Here's a new set of notes for you to add to your prized notebook. One of my coaching mentors gave these to me and I want to pass them along to you. Read through these and tell me what they mean to you."

The sheet of paper read:

Sustaining Excellence

- **Recommit Daily**
  Success is rented and rent is due every day.
  Ask: What am I choosing to commit to today?

- **Refine the Routine**
  What got you here won't always get you there.
  Ask: What needs to evolve in my preparation?

- **Reflect Deeper**
  Surface wins fade. Deep growth sticks.
  Ask: Who am I becoming through this process?

- **Reinvest in the Culture**
  Excellence isn't sustained alone. You must give it away.
  Ask: How am I helping others grow too?

Jai read through the notes slowly and nodded his head. "I used to think being great was hitting the big shot, scoring a lot of points, or winning a game."

He looked up from the paper and locked eyes with Coach Ellis.

"But I've learned so much the last few years from you and Coach Victor. I know greatness is more than that. It's doing the little things every day. It's in the moments that no one sees. Moments like this."

"I don't need to worry about being consistently great, but I need to be great at being consistent."

Coach Ellis extended his hand to lift Jai up off the floor.

"You're getting it, Jai. You've become a winner, but now you're becoming someone who knows how to keep winning. I'm learning this lesson right alongside of you. I think we are both stepping into our greatness."

As they walked toward the exit and out of the gym, Coach Ellis said one more important thing to Jai.

"Now that you've begun to grasp this, I want you to teach someone else. Go lead your teammates and bring them this newfound knowledge that you received. Our team is better because of you, and I'm excited to see how we sustain this."

"I'm ready, Coach!"

Jai was beginning to leave his legacy and was ready to pass it on.

TWENTY-FOUR
THE UNDENIABLE RISE

The team rallied for the remainder of the regular season. While there were still bumps in the road like late-game turnovers, missed free throws, and defensive lapses, they didn't unravel like they had earlier in the year. Something had shifted. The players weren't just talking about *Win One Won*, they were living it. They were showing up to practice early, holding each other accountable, and finding strength in the small, consistent wins that didn't show up on the stat sheet. The culture was changing, and with it, their confidence.

After finishing the regular season with a gritty win over the top seed, Jai and his teammates entered the conference tournament with a lot of momentum. Although the team believed, no one on the outside seemed to share that belief.

Analysts called them "overachievers." Headlines dismissed their chances. "Not built for March," one article read. "Lacking depth, lacking size." But inside the locker room, the noise didn't reach them. Coach Ellis had built something deeper. He had built belief.

He built belief by:

- Leaning into his team's identity.
- Stacking small wins.
- Speaking life into every person he encountered.
- Surrounding himself with people who were not "yes-men."
- Praising the moments when his team showed up the right way.

After all, what gets praised gets repeated.

They entered the tournament as the number four seed, an underdog with nothing to lose and everything to prove. Game by game, they knocked off the so-called favorites.

In the semifinals, they found themselves down by two with 4.6 seconds left. Coach Ellis calmly drew up the final play, trusting his players to execute. They did, and Jai delivered the assist on a buzzer-beating jumper that sent the crowd into a frenzy.

The conference championship game was their masterpiece. Poised, precise, and relentless, they played their most complete game of the year. Jai didn't have to score 30 to make an impact. He led with his voice, his defense, and his composure. Everyone contributed. Every player knew their role and played it with purpose.

When the final horn sounded, they had done it. The program's first-ever conference tournament championship. Their first automatic bid to the national tournament. A banner was coming, and history had been made.

While this all felt like a dream for Jai, he knew he was ready for the moment.

TWENTY-FIVE
LOVE, SERVE, COMPETE

J ust as the noise started to die down from their conference championship, Coach Ellis walked quietly to the front of the room, holding a whiteboard marker in his hand.

Without raising his voice, he wrote three words.

Love. Serve. Compete.

"Tonight, you made history," Coach Ellis said. "But what got us here is what will carry us forward."

He pointed to the board.

"*Love* means we stay present and connected. Don't miss these moments. Don't drift into anxiety about what's next. Love each other by being fully here. In every timeout. Every possession. Every huddle. We play *for* each other, not just with each other."

"*Serve* means you do your job. No shortcuts, no egos, no excuses. Set the screen. Sprint back. Make the extra pass. Be the guy who makes the guy next to you better. You serve your teammates by taking responsibility for your role and doing your job. Every rep, every play."

"A friend of mine summed it up best. He used to tell his team to be responsible to the element, which were their individual roles. And then they needed to be accountable to the mission, which were our overall team goals."

"*Compete* means we fight for more than stats or spotlight. We compete to make winning contagious. We dive on the floor, we high-five after mistakes, and we defend like it's the last possession of our lives. That's what makes this team different. We don't just play hard, we elevate the standard."

He paused, then added one more phrase beneath the three core words:

Win One Won.

"You know this. But right now, we have to *live* it with everything we've got. That's how we move from conference champions to national contenders. One moment at a time."

The players nodded. The conference championship trophy sat there on the bench. But they weren't looking at it anymore.

They were looking at the whiteboard.

They knew what mattered now.

It was on to the national tournament.

TWENTY-SIX
MARCHING FORWARD

The first round of the national tournament was a test of nerves and composure. It was the type of game that reminded everyone just how crazy March can be. The crowd was loud, the tension thick, and every possession felt like it carried the weight of the season. With the score tied and the clock winding down, the ball found Jai's hands. He had missed a few earlier shots that game, but none of it mattered now. He caught it, squared up, and let it fly.

The buzzer sounded. The shot dropped.

Pandemonium erupted.

People dream of moments like this, but to experience it was a whole different level. Jai had delivered in the biggest moment of his career, so far, and lifted his team into the second round. Madness.

But the next game wouldn't be decided by a single shot. It would be defined by grit. They faced a team that came out firing, capitalizing on every mistake and quickly jumping out to a nineteen-point lead. Things could've unraveled. In the past, they might have. But this was a different team now, fueled by the *Win One Won* mindset.

Jai rallied the group during a timeout, reminding them to stay in the fight. Possession by possession, stop by stop, they chipped away. It wasn't pretty, but it was personal. They clawed their way back, taking charges, diving for loose balls, and making the hustle plays that never show up in a box score. By the time the final buzzer sounded, they had erased the deficit and pulled off one of the gutsiest comebacks of the tournament.

The Sweet Sixteen and Elite Eight games were defensive battles. Offense was hard to come by, and both games tested their mental toughness. But Coach Ellis reminded them that momentum lives in the present. The next play was always the most important one. And they lived it, possessing a laser focus on defense, communicating, rotating, contesting every shot. They suffocated their opponents with effort and execution.

The Winner's Approach was no longer something they talked about. It was who they were.

And then, somehow, they were in the national semifinals.

Jai had never looked more locked in. From the opening tip, he controlled the tempo of the game. He picked apart the defense, made plays for others, and took over when his team needed him most. Scouts in the stands were scribbling notes furiously as he showed poise, leadership, and the kind of versatility that only comes from deep internal growth. He finished with one of the most complete performances of his career and carried his team to one more victory.

They had done the unthinkable.

One more game. One more opportunity. The national championship awaited.

MINDSET: WON

<u>**WON Mindset**</u>

"Won" isn't just the result. It's a mindset rooted in impact. It's about compounding success, sustaining excellence, and living a life of significance through who you've become and how you lead others.

Compounding Success

Winning isn't a one-time event. It's a daily decision. What you repeatedly do defines who you become. When you win the small moments, they add up to something greater. Celebrate the wins, big and small. But don't stop there. Share them. Pour into others. Make momentum contagious.

Ask yourself:

- What habit or wins am I compounding
  right now?
- Am I maximizing today to become better
  tomorrow?
- Who else am I elevating by sharing my growth?

Sustaining Excellence

Anyone can have a great day. Champions show up every day. Winning becomes a part of their identity and deeper purpose. Sustained excellence comes from systems, not moods. From humility and a deep commitment to growth. This phase isn't about chasing more, it's about protecting what got you here and elevating the standard.

Ask yourself:

- What systems keep me grounded in excellence?
- Where am I drifting from the habits that
  helped me win?
- How do I stay steady when the pressure or
  success increases?

Finding Significance

Success is what you accomplish. Significance is who you impact. It's about shifting from me to we, from performance to purpose. When your life multiplies leadership in others, you're building something that outlasts you. Your legacy isn't measured by the scoreboard, but by how many others you helped win.

Ask yourself:

- **Am I chasing trophies or am I creating ripple effects?**
- **Will people remember what I did or how I made them better?**
- **How can I serve beyond the moment and lead beyond myself?**

PART FIVE
LEGACY AND SIGNIFICANCE
THIS IS WHAT IT'S ALL ABOUT

TWENTY-SEVEN
PRESENCE OVER PRESSURE

The practices leading up to the championship game felt different. They were sharper. While energy filled the room, the team was focused . . . and a little quieter. Not a scared quiet, but a laser-focused, ready-to-win-the moment kind of quiet. They had earned their shot and weren't going to spoil this opportunity.

Normally, teams would feel pressure in this situation. Jai and his teammates, though, felt peace. Jai's presence had rubbed off on the rest of the team, and they realized that their preparation led to their consistency . . . and they were ready.

The night before the championship game, the team had one final shoot-around in the arena. Jai was walking out of the tunnel and paused. He soaked in the moment. The empty seats. The bright lights. The smell in the air. He had dreamt of this moment, and he was finally here.

Coach Ellis wasn't far behind him and stopped to stand next to him.

"How are you feeling, Jai?"

"Incredible, Coach. I'm just trying to take it all in. I thought I would be more nervous, but I'm not. I know I'm ready."

Coach Ellis smiled and nodded in agreement. "Yes, you are. You've put the work in. You've been consistent. This moment isn't too big for you anymore; you were built for this."

The next morning, the team gathered in the hotel ballroom for one last film session to prepare for the game. After the coaches showed the clips and talked through the scouting report, Coach Ellis stood at the front of the room and addressed the team. His speech wasn't anything earth-shattering, but it meant more and had a purpose behind it.

"This is not an accident that we are here. We embraced the process and went on this adventure step-by-step—together.

We showed up every single day with the Winner's Approach. And while we were preparing for a championship all season, we became champions by the way we loved each other, served each other, and competed for each other. Even when things were hard, we locked in and did the right thing. Our story is already written, and tomorrow is just the final chapter."

The team was all in. They truly believed that they had done everything they needed to do to be ready for this game.

Coach Ellis asked the team if anyone wanted to say anything before they turned in for the night.

Jai stood up and walked to the front of the room. His body language screamed steadiness and confidence.

"We bought in. We trusted each other. This team is special. We aren't perfect, but through the bad games, injuries, and the tough moments, we stayed together. We lived up to our standard every day. And guess what? Tomorrow we get to play in a national championship game! We are ready to win it. I know this because we've already won all the moments that mattered. Let's bring it in, boys."

The team huddled around Jai and put their hands in. "1, 2, 3 . . . WIN ONE WON!"

Before the team checked out of the hotel to get on the bus to head to the arena, Coach Ellis knocked on Jai's door.

"What's up, Jai? Just wanted to check in with you before we headed out. Is that okay?"

"Of course, Coach," Jai said.

They sat down on the couch, and Coach Ellis looked at Jai and said, "You know I'm proud of you, right?"

Jai smiled from ear to ear. "Yeah, I know."

Coach continued, "Not just because you're a great player, but because of who you've become. You've become a great young man. You've realized that your significance is in how you impact others, not just what you achieve personally. I love how you've shown up day after day even when no one was applauding you."

"Thanks, Coach," Jai said. "That means a lot."

"Today, I want you to go be you," Coach Ellis said. "You don't need to be perfect, and I don't want you to force anything. Just go lead your team and compete hard. Love it and leave it all on the floor."

"I will. Coach, thank you for believing in me," Jai said. "You've helped me grow so much and become who I'm supposed to be. I thank God for you every day."

Coach Ellis nodded and gave him a hug. "I guess we've already won. Let's go do this."

The team went to board the bus and head to the arena. There was a feeling of anticipation and nervousness the air. The players were ready and the coaching staff made their final preparations for the game. Coach Ellis gave some final words of inspiration, but he knew his guys were already motivated because of who they were as people. He wrapped it up and walked out. It was time to go.

Jai took a deep breath as he looked at himself in the mirror before heading to the court. He didn't check his hair or fix his headband, but looked himself in the eyes to give one final message.

"To win the moment, you need to be in the moment, Jai. Win the moment. Win the day. Win One . . . and you've already Won."

One final deep breath was all he needed before walking out to the energized arena. He was ready to go. A fire was lit inside of him, and he was poised to perform at a high level in the biggest game of his life.

TWENTY-EIGHT
THE DEFINING MOMENT

This was it. The championship game. For all the ups and downs this season had brought, it was all culminating in the biggest test of the year. Jai was locked in.

Jai's leadership had impacted his team in significant ways throughout the season. Everyone was looking up to him to do it one more time. Normally, Jai would feel enormous pressure in situations like this, the weight of the world on his shoulders. But not this time. While there were still nerves, Jai felt a sense of calm and composure. His growth in *Win One Won* had made a difference.

From the opening tip, both teams came ready to play. Their opponent was scrappy, and they played a fast and furious defense that threw Jai and his team off rhythm. Jai missed his first three shots of the game and was visibly frustrated. As someone who felt prepared before the game, he quickly began to feel the gravity pushing down on him. The lights were brighter than ever, and the fans' anxious energy was evident.

But this wasn't Jai from years past.

In years past, Jai would've folded. He would've let the pressure get to him. He would've snapped and put the blame on his teammates.

But this version of Jai was living in the *Win One Won* mentality.

Instead of forcing shots or folding in the moment, Jai reset his focus elsewhere. He played lockdown defense and made it his mission to stop his opponent from scoring. Not only did he guard his yard, but he elevated the energy of his teammates through his communication and effort. He ripped rebounds out of the air, sprinted to help up a fallen teammate, and even found the open man for a big shot right before halftime.

He wasn't scoring like he normally did, but the impact he was making on the game was turning heads.

With under a minute to go in the game, Jai would make the play that would be remembered the most. It wasn't a dunk. It wasn't a big three-pointer. It was a selfless and gritty hustle play, diving on the floor for a loose ball to give his team an extra possession. He called a timeout and gave Coach Ellis the opportunity to draw up a set play.

———

Jai was leading. He was living out the list of 10 things leaders do. Leaders:

1. Lead with their presence.
2. Shift their focus from self to the team.
3. Respond, don't react.
4. Elevate energy through their effort.
5. Communicate with clarity and confidence.
6. Make momentum plays.
7. Create space and opportunity for others to succeed.
8. Finish with purpose.
9. Find their hope in identity, not outcome.
10. Leave a legacy beyond the final score.

———

At this moment, Jai shifted all the momentum in favor of his team, and they were poised to finish this game. The team came out of the timeout and executed to perfection. One of Jai's teammates hit a corner three, which would be the dagger sealing their victory.

When that final buzzer sounded, confetti fell from the rafters, and it was pure bedlam in the arena.

They were national champions.

But more importantly, Jai realized his growth as a leader was more than talent. It was about his presence and purpose.

TWENTY-NINE
FINDING SIGNIFICANCE

The locker room was almost empty now. The celebration had ended. The media interviews were complete. Jai's ears were still humming from the sound of the final buzzer and the chaos of the night, but he sat in silence, the last one to leave the room.

Jai sat there alone, jersey damp with sweat, with his eyes looking to the sky. He had a piece of the net tied around his hat and the national championship trophy still sitting on the bench beside him.

He put his hand on the trophy and took a long look at it. This was it. This is what everyone plays the game for. But in that moment he had a soft grin appear on his face. He didn't feel shock or disbelief, but rather clarity. He knew it wasn't about the trophy after all.

Just then, Coach Ellis quietly stepped into the locker room.

"Hey Coach," Jai said. "You know, I always thought winning a championship would give me a sense of validation, like I'd proved something to everyone, but I don't feel that at all."

Coach Ellis was caught a little off guard, but was curious to hear where Jai was going with this.

"What does it feel like then?"

Jai smiled bigger than he'd ever smiled before. "It feels like purpose!"

Coach smiled and gave Jai a big hug. "I'm so proud of you, Jai. That's what this is all about."

Jai sat back down and leaned forward. "I can't stop thinking about this adventure I've been on the last few years: Coach Victor. The early-morning practices. The journaling. The nights I couldn't sleep. The mindset shifts I had to make. I never understood why some things were happening to me .. . but I see it now.

"I see how winning the moment led to winning the day. I was able to own my adversity and overcome setbacks. The more days I stacked, the better I became.

"Between you and Coach Victor, you both taught me how to love, serve, and compete with humility. You showed me that success was great, but significance was even better. You never let the scoreboard define me. You taught me my identity could be rooted in something greater."

Coach Ellis leaned in. "You were always capable, but your character growth has allowed you to get to where you're at today. You've taken the right approach and you've built the right habits, and now you're a champion. But even more significant than that, you're a leader who is going to build more champions."

THIRTY
THE REAL REWARD

The next day, the university and the entire city celebrated the championship with a parade. The streets were lined with fans who had waited their entire lives for this day! The local fire department passed out candy as the team was led by a police escort. As the buses passed by, they came to the final destination where there was a stage set up. The entire team wanted Jai to be the one to speak to the enormous crowd.

"I know this championship means so much to so many, and we are extremely proud of what we did. But today, I want to remind you of who we became.

"We didn't win this championship because we had more talent. It wasn't because of one shot or one moment. It was because we made an intentional decision to win each moment, every day. We stacked small wins every day, and it led to big results. We won because we stayed locked in, even when things didn't seem too good. We responded in those moments; we didn't react. We won because we loved each other enough to hold each other accountable. We won because we served each other by doing our jobs. We won because we competed with joy and purpose.

"This trophy is great, but it's not the ultimate reward. This team became different and grew into something special. That is the real reward."

Jai took a pause and looked around at his teammates surrounding him on the stage.

"Every rep. Every tough practice. Every rough stretch when we had to move on to the next play. Every journal entry. Every hard conversation. We made a lot of sacrifices for each other. But it was worth it.

"Our greatest victory was learning how to *Win One Won*, and now we get to go help others do the same! Isn't God good?!"

After all the cheers and all the fanfare, Jai was tired. He got back home late that night and fell into his bed. Before he closed his eyes, he grabbed his journal one last time. He clicked open his pen and flipped over to the last clean page in the book and wrote:

"Success is when you win. Significance is when you help others win too."

He smiled and closed the notebook.

Jai had won. Not just the game, but his moment, his mindset, and his mission.

He knew the next chapter of his life—one filled with purpose, impact, and legacy—was just beginning.

ABOUT THE AUTHOR

Andrew Wingreen is a college basketball coach, dynamic speaker, and the creator of the *Win One Won* philosophy, a transformational framework built to help high performers win the moment, win the day, and ultimately win in life. With over fifteen years of coaching experience, Andrew has developed leaders on and off the court by instilling values of purpose, preparation, and perseverance.

After overcoming personal adversity, including major heart surgeries, Andrew became deeply committed to helping others not only succeed, but live with greater significance. He is a follower of Jesus and his approach to leadership is practical, powerful, and heart-centered, blending elite performance with character development. Through *Win One Won*, he equips athletes, teams, and organizations to build championship habits, embrace adversity, and create a culture of sustained excellence.

Andrew lives in Florida with his wife and daughters, where he continues to coach, speak, and inspire the next generation of leaders.

instagram.com/coachwingreen

x.com/coachwingreen

facebook.com/coachwingreen

tiktok.com/@coachwingreenspeaks

linkedin.com/in/andrew-wingreen-a97856270

ACKNOWLEDGMENTS

This book wouldn't exist without the people who braved this adventure with me.

First and foremost, **Jesus**—thank you for calling me up to something bigger than myself. This book wouldn't have been written if you didn't have a purpose for it. My prayer is that people will come to know you and find their true identity in you.

To my wife, **Julie**—thank you for being in it with me every step of the way. You read, edited, offered ideas, and enhanced this book in ways only you could. You believed in this message from day one and never stopped cheering me on, even when life threw curveballs. Your steady support and constant smile mean the world to me.

To my daughters, **Aaliya and Rylee**—thank you for always being creative, curious, and honest. Your input gave me fresh ideas and reminded me how important it is to make complex lessons simple. You've helped me more than you know.

To my **mom and dad**—you've always believed in me. Your encouragement through every season of life made this possible. You've been my biggest fans since the beginning, and I'm forever grateful.

To my **coaching staff and team**—you live out the *Win One Won* mindset every day. You inspire me to show up, lead better, and keep learning. This philosophy wouldn't be real without your example.

And to the **coaches who've mentored, challenged, and shaped me**—many of the stories in this book exist because of your leadership. Thank you for sharing your wisdom, trusting me to be a part of your teams, and helping me grow into the person and coach I am today.

This book is for all of you.

ADDITIONAL RESOURCES

Your journey doesn't end here. If *Win One Won* resonated with you, here are a few ways to go deeper and bring the mindset to your team, organization, or personal life:

Keynote Speaking

Looking for a powerful and practical keynote that connects with athletes, leaders, or teams? I speak on topics like leadership, mindset, habits, and high performance, all rooted in the *Win One Won* philosophy.

To inquire about booking, visit:
www.coachwingreen.com/speaking

Leadership Training, Team Workshops, & One-on-One Coaching

Whether you're a coach, business leader, educator, or athlete, I offer customized training experiences that help teams build culture, strengthen leadership, and execute with clarity.

Learn more at:

www.coachwingreen.com/speaking

Digital Resources & Coaching Tools

Access exclusive PDFs, planners, and more designed to help you implement the *Win One Won* approach in your everyday leadership.

Browse resources at:

www.coachwingreen.com/resources

Join the Win One Won Community

Get leadership insights, free tools, and early access to new projects by joining the newsletter:

www.coachwingreen.com